"*Refuse to Do Nothing* offers the new a[...] careful foundation for understanding and evaluating [...] battle and make her effort count. The authors build a solid case for individual responsibility in our own backyard. Additionally, the reflective exercises provide opportunity for a meaningful pause that fosters sustainable commitments rather than emotional highs that fade with time and distance. This is the small group study guide that I've been looking for and will recommend to students, community service groups and churches."

SANDIE MORGAN, director, Global Center for Women & Justice

"Kim and Shayne exemplify a long tradition of ordinary citizens refusing to sit on the sidelines while the poor suffer. They are relentless and an inspiration for us all."

JUSTIN DILLON, director, Call + Response, and CEO, Slavery Footprint

"Reader, you were made for this. Where you are today—your home, job, community, life—is exactly where God will use you to set captives free. In these pages Shayne Moore and Kimberly McOwen Yim invite you to join the particularly Christian work of ending human slavery. On each page you'll be saying to yourself, 'I can do this.' Thanks be to God."

MARGOT STARBUCK, author, *Small Things with Great Love*

"*Refuse to Do Nothing* is not a comfortable read. It is intended to open our eyes to the brutal world of human trafficking, to break our hearts over what grieves God's heart and to make us uneasy if we do nothing. I pray that God will use this powerful and practical book to ignite in us a fierce resolve to engage this battle and that we will not rest until the last captive is freed!"

CAROLYN CUSTIS JAMES, author, *Half the Church*

"Shayne and Kim have found their voice in helping us recognize where our worlds may have grown small, and how, through practical choices and conversations, we can thrive as conduits of change as we make justice an everyday habit."

BETTY ANN BOEVING, founder of the Bay Area Anti-Trafficking Coalition

REFUSE TO DO NOTHING

FINDING YOUR POWER TO
ABOLISH MODERN-DAY SLAVERY

SHAYNE MOORE AND
KIMBERLY McOWEN YIM

Foreword by Elisa Morgan

IVP Books

An imprint of InterVarsity Press
Downers Grove, Illinois

InterVarsity Press
P.O. Box 1400, Downers Grove, IL 60515-1426
World Wide Web: www.ivpress.com
E-mail: email@ivpress.com

InterVarsity Press® is the book-publishing division of InterVarsity Christian Fellowship/USA®, a
movement of students and faculty active on campus at hundreds of universities, colleges and schools of
nursing in the United States of America, and a member movement of the International Fellowship of
Evangelical Students. For information about local and regional activities, write Public Relations Dept.,
InterVarsity Christian Fellowship/USA, 6400 Schroeder Rd., P.O. Box 7895, Madison, WI 53707-7895,
or visit the IVCF website at <www.intervarsity.org>.

All Scripture quotations, unless otherwise indicated, are taken from THE HOLY BIBLE, NEW
INTERNATIONAL VERSION®, NIV® Copyright © 1973, 1978, 1984, 2011 by Biblica, Inc.™ Used by
permission. All rights reserved worldwide.

While all stories in this book are true, some names and identifying information in this book have been
changed to protect the privacy of the individuals involved.

Cover design: Cindy Kiple
Interior design: Beth Hagenberg
Images: Nick Purser/Getty Images

ISBN 978-0-8308-4302-2

Printed in the United States of America ∞

Library of Congress Cataloging-in-Publication Data
A catalog record for this book is available from the Library of Congress.

P	18	17	16	15	14	13	12	11	10	9	8	7	6	5	4	3	2	1
Y	28	27	26	25	24	23	22	21	20	19	18	17	16	15	14	13		

We dedicate this book to our children:
John David, Greta, Thomas, Malia and Scotty.

May they live in a world free of slavery.
We also dedicate these words to the abolitionists
we have met along the way who fight for freedom
on behalf of the silent slaves in our midst.

Contents

The world can no longer be left to only diplomats, politicians and business leaders. They have done the best they could, no doubt. But this is an age for spiritual heroes—a time for men and women to be heroic in their faith and in spiritual character and power. The greatest danger to the Christian church today is that of pitching its message too low.

DALLAS WILLARD, *THE SPIRIT OF THE DISCIPLINES*

◆　◆　◆

I can't stress enough the importance of prayer. . . .
Pray for the victims and the efforts to eradicate slavery.

REP CHRIS SMITH, U.S. HOUSE OF REPRESENTIVES

◆　◆　◆

Lord, may I be an Abolitionist
Oppression's deadly foe;
In God's great strength will I resist
And lay the monster low.
In God's great name do I demand
To all be freedom given;
That peace and joy may fill the land
And songs go up to heaven.

ANONYMOUS PRAYER

Foreword

The doorbell rang. In my corner of suburbia and at my post-children stage of life, no one really comes to the door unless it's with a delivery. I wondered who was sending me what and rose from my desk in my home office.

Opening the door I sensed immediately it was a door-to-door salesperson of some sort. Magazines? Candy? Window washing? I wasn't interested and cued up my rote response. "Thanks but we're set . . ."

The young man held out his hand with a card. "I'm Joseph . . . I'm selling magazines . . ."

I looked him over as I took the card. Late teens? His clothes were low-rent but clean and neat. His face: pale and thin. He stuttered a bit as he flipped through the booklet of magazines offered for purchase.

I didn't have time for this.

And then I remembered. Just a few weeks prior, I'd driven across town to hear a local leader talk about sex trafficking. The topic had intrigued me and because I'd gradually begun to allow that such realities might exist in my world, I accepted the invitation and put the event on my calendar. Seated before a fireplace, holding a cup of coffee, I was dumbfounded at the reported number of children, teens and young people imprisoned in trafficking in my hometown of Denver, Colorado. Modern-day slavery.

The speaker explained, "Everyday businesses like massage parlors and nail salons frequently make use of trafficked individuals. Whole teams of door-to-door salespeople are actually trafficked children who have been duped into working for housing and food just to survive."

Door-to-door salespeople.

I looked at Joseph again. "How is this business working for you?" I asked. He paused, clearly not accustomed to such a question. "Are you paid with food and housing in return for your sales? Have you sold much today?"

Joseph swallowed, looked over his shoulder and then dipped his voice in response, "No ma'am, I haven't sold much and I'm kinda nervous about that. Yeah, this is how I survive."

I remembered the speaker had offered a phone number—the national hotline for sex trafficked individuals. I'd written it down and put it somewhere on my desk. Asking Joseph to wait a minute, I hurried to get the sticky and returned to the door, holding it out to him.

"Joseph, there's another way to live. Keep this. Call the number when you're ready. There is help."

It wasn't much, what I did. Maybe it was kind of a coward's action, an arm's distance effort as I've never seen Joseph again. But I acted because I've grown to understand that action is what matters.

About a decade ago, God dead-ended me into a passage in the Gospel of Mark (14:1-8) where I discovered a story that changed my life. Jesus received Mary's gift of nard and responded, "She did what she could." These five words grabbed me and haven't let go. I don't have to do it all to make a difference. I simply need to act. To put feet on my faith. I can make a difference in the everyday. Apologizing to a coworker for a tacky comment. Taking time for coffee with a stressed-out mom. Sponsoring education and relief for a child in a Third-World country. Attending a seminar on trafficking.

When I do what I could . . . I can change the world.

And so can you.

Read this book. The topic is daunting, I know. Just turn this page—and then the next. Keep turning the pages until you've read all the way through. And then, do something. Respond to the reflections at the end of each chapter. Tear out the websites and tape them on your computer screen. Make a pad of stickies with the sex-trafficking hotline number and have them at your ready.

Refuse to do nothing. Mary did what she could, and Jesus said it was a beautiful thing. Do what you can.

Is that your doorbell?

Elisa Morgan

Introduction

Shayne's Story

I was happily and exhaustingly deep in the trenches of motherhood. I spent my days corralling John David, at that time an energetic six-year-old. Cuddling with Greta, a curly-headed three-year-old. Enmeshed in the demands of Thomas, my seven-month-old.

Those long, blurry days of new motherhood found me with uncombed hair pulled off my face in a lopsided ponytail. Comfortable clothes, not trendy fashion, was the go-to every morning, and more than likely the tee shirt I threw on, the one I grabbed off the floor, had spit-up on it—which I would notice later in the day and do nothing about.

My biggest concerns were making sure everyone was safe, fed and (somewhat) clean. Those were the days of finding Greta a block down the street on her Big Wheel, wearing only a diaper, having gotten up on her own from a nap and decided to go for a spin. Plastic dinosaurs dominated every windowsill and open space. For years I lived with a screeching raptor; John David's characterization of prehistoric times was very convincing. It was a monumental feat back then to find a clean onesie and a sippy cup that didn't leak. Going to Target with no kids was a luxurious outing.

I loved my life. I loved being a mom.

Through middle school, high school, college and eighteen years of marriage I have lived in the same town, moved in the same

The Moores, visiting a coffee farm in rural Honduras

space. I am comfortable in my surroundings, my cocoon of friends and family. Everywhere I go around town I see a smiling familiar face. If I am ever in need I am warmly taken care of with meals, childcare, snow removal, you name it.

In the midst of my full mommy life, sometimes in the rare quiet and reflective moments, something nagged my mind and heart, but I was good at ignoring it. For years I pushed it away. Just do another load of laundry. Run to the store. Clean off the desk. Bath time, nap time, dinner time. But there was no shaking the memory of a time when I imagined something different for my life, when the adventurist in me exerted herself.

After graduating from Wheaton College I moved to South Central Los Angeles to be an inner-city schoolteacher and missionary. Six months after the 1992 L.A. riots, when buildings were still burned out and windows smashed, I started teaching seventh- and eighth-grade English and history and had the immense honor of leading a discipleship group for my students. Together we survived South Central, the Northridge earthquake and the tough years of middle school. I am forever endeared to this slice of my history and these students.

My time as a missionary stretched and molded me. Several nights each week the echoing sound of gunfire disturbed my attic bedroom. My roommate and I would turn the lights off and watch the parade of women and men flowing in and out of the crack house behind us. Hearing distant automatic weapon drive-bys and constant car alarms was very different from falling asleep to the distant sound of the train rumbling through downtown Wheaton, Illinois.

The years in the inner city challenged my thinking on poverty, education, race and faith. I lived and worked with people from many faith traditions and ethnicities. It was a time I remember as being alive. It felt as if I were on a fast-moving train racing toward God's purposes for our world.

And then I got married. And moved home. And had babies.

I fell into a suburban stupor.

Sometimes I struggled. The nagging thought I was good at pushing away—it would sneak up and haunt me. I had become everything I'd made fun of. I was a soccer mom. I drove a minivan. I schlepped baby gear. I was consumed with potty training and nap schedules.

I wish someone had assured me this was a good and normal progression of life. I wish I knew then what I know now—that being a big thinker for God's purposes in the world and being a soccer mom are not mutually exclusive. When you have babies your world gets very small—this is appropriate and as it should be. As those babies grow and move out into the world, so will we as their mothers.

That moving out into the world will look different for different women. For me it took the shape of a global movement. In 2003 I heard a presentation in my hometown that changed the trajectory of my life.

I learned about the realities of the HIV-AIDS pandemic in sub-Saharan Africa and about the staggering realities of other mothers and families just like my own. At that time it was projected that by 2010 there would be twenty-five million orphans due to AIDS. Nine thousand Africans were dying every day from a preventable disease. I learned the mind-numbing reality that the number one cause of death in children under the age of five in Africa is diarrhea: while I can just run a block to Walgreens and get Pedialyte, other mothers are watching their children die.

I woke up from my suburbia stupor. I couldn't shake God's voice telling me to pay attention to these things, even if at the time I had no idea what, as a stay-at-home mom, I could possibly do about any of it. The harsh realities of my counterparts in the world were hard to accept. I was reminded of everything I had been, everything I wanted to be—and what I was now. I was challenged to stop feeling sorry for myself by the perceived limitations of my life, and to move beyond myself and my family's needs—to take risks and act.

My mother's heart expanded, making room to care for more than the adorable people at my feet. I found my solidarity with women, mothers and families worldwide. I began to educate myself and others, and over time I found communities of like-minded people from all walks of life who work together for change.

I found that changing the world happens right where we are. It can be small changes in thinking and acting that end up having snowball effects and bringing the kingdom of God here and now. In the midst of motherhood, I slowly opened up my world to the possibilities of being a change agent within my generation. I traveled, blogged, even wrote a book—all from within the comfortable confines of my suburban life.

My kids are older now. Sippy cups and strollers have been replaced with iPhones and driving lessons. The past few years my non-mommy time has been spent speaking, writing and trying to educate others about what I've learned and witnessed since writing my first book, *Global Soccer Mom: Changing the World Is Easier Than You Think.* My efforts to be a global thinker and engage issues of our generation have spilled to my children and how they think and act in the world. I have come to see my waking up to being a global thinker as my biggest accomplishment and greatest satisfaction as a mother.

When my coauthor and friend, Kimberly McOwen Yim, first reached out to me, I was familiar with the desperation and heartbreak I heard in her voice. I had felt the same at the beginning of my journey. Kim shared what she was learning about the realities of modern-day slavery, and I immediately saw the connection with projects I had been involved with that addressed extreme poverty, HIV-AIDS and women's rights in the developing world.

As with many global issues, modern-day slavery is daunting and overwhelming. As I watched Kim work to educate her local community and heard her talk passionately about what she was doing, I consistently encouraged her to broaden her voice and her reach through more writing and speaking. I even dragged Kim to her computer one afternoon, despite her doubts, and we set up her blog, Abolitionist Mama.

Kim and I commiserated and learned from one another. We connected with like-minded women who share our heart for the world and who are also on this journey of working out what we can do about modern-day slavery. As time went on, we knew we needed to write a book together. The question we wrestled with the most was how two ordinary moms from middle America could tackle this topic and do it any justice—could we make any kind of meaningful dent?

We were unsure. But we knew we needed to start.

As you will see, Kim is persistent. And as she reminds me, so is slavery. So we do what we can. We start where we are. And slowly, but with real results, together we change the world.

Kim's Story

Comfortable, safe, predictable and *loved* would describe my life in my little beach town of San Clemente, California, where the city's motto is "Spanish village by the sea" and "The world's best climate" is the message on many license plate covers. Like Shayne, I still live in my hometown. I briefly left San Clemente to attend Westmont College in Santa Barbara, California, and later in my twenties I moved to Newport Beach, California. (Both also beach cities. There's a pattern.) There is a lot of comfort living in a community where people know you and still love you. My family still attends the church I grew up in, and my kids are surrounded by the love of grandparents, aunts and uncles, all who also live in San Clemente. I have a sweet life.

Prior to having kids I taught everyone's favorite subject: seventh-grade English. My love of learning eventually brought me to Fuller Seminary where I took my leisurely time (ten years) earning a master's degree. I've had the opportunity to travel a bit and have been on a handful of missions trips, but basically my life's mantra has been "safety first."

I considered myself a fairly good person. Not perfect but good: an at-least-I-tried kind of person. I was a good stay-at-home mom of sweet, good kids. I tried to be a supportive wife. I was a faithful churchgoer, supporting my local church and other charities my husband and I cared about. I volunteered when I could and loved participating in other mom-type groups. I might have considered

Yim family

myself, relatively speaking, "good people." But there is no way I ever considered myself standing in a position of power.

A statement by Gary Haugen, the founder and president of International Justice Mission, has come to be foundational to my journey in becoming a modern-day abolitionist:

> Truth compels people of goodwill to act; and because all that is necessary for the triumph of evil is for good people to do nothing, the end is near for the perpetrators of injustice when the truth compels good people to do something, especially good people in places of power.[1]

A few years ago I would have read this and thought he must be addressing ethical politicians, charismatic pastors or spiritual celebrities. I have noticed a trend of cause-oriented businesses emerging and actors using their platform to raise money for causes they care about. But I never considered myself "good people in places of power" because I didn't think I had power.

Oh, I might have had power over when our kids went to bed (most mothers would agree that this is power very tenuously held). I might have had some power over my family's spending or the food my family ate. But I saw those things as my responsibilities as a good mother, not as power.

Injustice has been around for a while: birthed by the murder of Abel by his brother Cain. I have always known that millions of people die because of AIDS, war, oppressive leadership and other horrible injustices. I have always read my Bible, gone to church and tried to be kind to others, but I honestly don't know why the injustice in the world never moved me to action.

Then one day I saw a film that showed me not only how slavery still existed in our world but that a response was needed to end it. My heart broke. I lost sleep. I found myself both sad and angry for many months.

At first I thought I was alone in my heartbreak, but thanks to social media I learned there were other ordinary mothers like me whose hearts were breaking over the injustices of the world. Over Facebook I reconnected with an old college friend, Shayne, who was just such a like-minded, brokenhearted mom.

My mantra of "safety first" has shifted a bit, but not all of a sudden; becoming an abolitionist has been a slow and winding path. Finding my place, where I could make a meaningful difference, has taken time and energy. I learned that true safety only comes in obedience to where the Lord leads you.

But I get ahead of myself. Let us tell you our story.

Mama,
Slavery Ended with Abraham Lincoln

Kimberly McOwen Yim

When the true history of the antislavery cause
shall be written, women will occupy a large space in its pages;
for the cause of the slave has been peculiarly woman's cause.

FREDERICK DOUGLASS

"Scotty, I asked you to find your backpack!" I holler as I shove my ponytail in a baseball cap. "Hurry! Get in the car! We're going to be late!"

Despite my best efforts, Mondays are always chaotic. When my husband takes the kids to school, they're somehow always early. But with me—we just barely get there on time.

As I climb in the car I catch a glimpse of the kitchen counter through the screen door. "Malia! Your lunch. It's on the counter." I gesture dramatically. "Go get it!"

The sun is shining brightly as we drive down the long hill leading to the coast and the kids' school. I have never tired of looking at the Pacific Ocean; I love to see how the weather changes its color each day.

"Okay, Scotty. Do you remember your lunch number? Remember—it's pizza day. Make sure to raise your hand so Mrs. Becerra knows to count you in the list for kids who are buying lunch today."

"I don't like to buy lunch anymore," Malia jibes.

"You did when you were in kindergarten." I pull down the rearview mirror to give her the stinkeye. "Scotty, pizza day is always fun."

My phone rings. "Hey, Julie, how are you? . . . Yeah . . . Uh-huh . . . No, I haven't touched base with her yet. I will . . . Okay, yes. I'm planning on it. I'll bring the materials tonight. Lisa is joining us tonight as well. I'll call you later. I gotta go. I'm at the kids' school."

I pull into a coveted space along the park across the street from the school. The kids tumble out of the car, and we walk the rest of the way. "Remember, I'm not picking you up from school this afternoon. Grandma is, okay?"

Malia struggles with her roller backpack, trying to pull it across the grass. "Why?"

"Remember, I told you. I'm going to a conference. Grandma knows where to meet you."

Malia persisted, "What kind of conference, Mom?"

In a few hours I'll be headed to Carlsbad, California, for the first Global Forum on Human Trafficking. Sponsored by the Not For Sale Campaign and Manpower, Inc., it will be the first conference I attend on the subject of human trafficking. I'm hoping to learn more about this issue that recently broke my heart.

Scotty and I push our way through the small crowd outside his classroom to the sign-in table. "Scotty, here. Sign your name." I say to Malia over my shoulder, "It's a conference on slavery."

Kind of a big thing to drop on a third-grader moments before school starts.

Malia looks at me thoughtfully. Then, with an air of first-born authority, she says, "Mama, slavery ended with Abraham Lincoln."

The five-minute bell rings, saving me from having to craft a response.

"We'll talk about it later. There's your bell. Run to class. Love you."

◆ ◆ ◆

Despite our age difference and different levels of formal education, Malia and I were not that far apart in our understanding of what's going on in our world. Until recently I too believed slavery ended with the Emancipation Proclamation and the end of the trans-Atlantic African slave trade. I only recently learned that there are millions of people enslaved in our world today.

When I did discover the extent of modern-day slavery, I became sick, sad and furious. The lioness within me awoke hungry for justice. I began to see myself aligned with passionate abolitionist women from two hundred years ago. Women like Lucretia Mott and the Grimke sisters, who did not stand on the sidelines but actively participated and provided much leadership in the anti-slavery movement of the mid-1800s. They organized female abolitionist societies because during that time women and men were not allowed to participate in the same groups—even anti-slavery groups. These women organized boycotts of slave-made goods such as cotton and sugar, mobilizing thousands of women. Through their leadership other ordinary women began to see that despite not having a vote or a voice outside their homes, their actions and contributions were needed to end slavery in the United States.

I desperately wanted to connect with other women who had that same passion for our world today. I didn't know what I was going to do about it or what it would look like in my life, but I refused to do nothing. I clenched the steering wheel with resolve. In the quiet of my car I became an abolitionist.

I have come to believe that it is not by chance that I was born

"Slave–Free."

in the United States at this time in history. I have personal power many people in the world do not. I believe women like me—women with freedom, liberty and opportunity—have an obligation to speak into our generation on behalf of those in the world who do not have a voice: those targeted, exploited and held against their will.

I believe each of us has something meaningful to contribute in the fight against global slavery. Regardless of our age, circumstance and season of life, we all can do our part. We are good people in places of power, and as such we must work together with resilience, faith and courage. We must fight against indifference—the feeling that there's nothing we can do about problems "over there." We must claim our power to set the captives free.

Reflect

1. Think about the idea of "good people in places of power." What does this mean to you?

2. In what ways are you a good person in a place (or places) of power?

2

We've Done This Before

Shayne Moore

*The abolitionists succeeded because
they mastered one challenge that still faces anyone
who cares about social and economic justice: drawing
connections between the near and the distant.*

ADAM HOCHSCHILD, *BURY THE CHAINS*

Slavery isn't new. The pursuit of wealth has resulted in the enslavement and exploitation of others since the beginning of time. Unlike in the past, however, slavery is now illegal everywhere in the world.

Even so, there are more people enslaved today than there were during the entire trans-Atlantic African slave trade that ran from the sixteenth to the nineteenth century. The widely accepted estimate of number of slaves in the world today is twenty-seven million people.[1] Eighty percent are women and children.[2]

Picture every person in Los Angeles, New York City and Chicago. Now picture them as slaves.

The institutionalized African slave trade we learned about in history classes has been abolished. Yet modern-day slavery is the fastest-growing criminal industry in the world, with profits of more than $32 billion—roughly the same as Exxon Mobil.[3] Companies the size of Exxon Mobil are eager for you to see them, and they are accountable to the regulation of the governments of their host countries. Modern-day slavery violates the laws of every country in the world, and the people who traffick other human beings are thrilled when nobody notices.

Criminals who engage in human trafficking have created a well-organized, elusive international market for the trade of human beings based on high profits and cheap labor. Pimps and mafia lords have figured out it is cheaper to sell a person than to sell a drug. A drug pusher sells a drug once; once it's sold, he has to replenish his supply. A pimp or slave owner "sells" each woman over and over again, profiting again and again from the exploitation.

These realities are sickening and daunting. How do we wrap our hearts and minds around the reality that there are people suffering in slavery more now than ever in the history of the world?

We can be informed immediately of breaking news anywhere in the world. We sit at our TVs or computer screens and consume mass amounts of information daily. The challenge for good and thoughtful people of our generation is to not merely consume information but learn how to act and engage with what we learn.

You may have heard the terms "human trafficking" or "modern-day slavery," but only in passing. "Human trafficking," as we've learned, is the process of enslaving and physically moving a person against their will. It is the modern-day slave trade. The United Nations Convention against Transnational Organized Crime defines human trafficking as

> the recruitment, transportation, harboring, or receipt of persons by means of the threat or use of force or other forms of coercion, of abduction, of fraud, of deception, of the abuse

of power or of a position of vulnerability or of the giving or receiving of payments or benefits to achieve the consent of a person having control over another person, for the purpose of exploitation. Exploitation shall include at a minimum, the exploitation of the prostitutions of others or other forms of sexual exploitation, forced labor or services, slavery or practices similar to slavery, servitude or the removal of organs.[4]

The U.S. State Department's characterization of slavery, based on the Trafficking Victims Protection Act of 2000

- The recruitment, harboring, transportation, provision or obtaining of a person for labor or services, through the use of force, fraud or coercion, for the purpose of subjection to involuntary servitude, peonage, debt bondage or slavery. Evidence of these practices can be seen in agriculture, the restaurant business, mining, nail salons, hair-braiding businesses, domestic servitude and a variety of types of manufacturing.

- A commercial sex act induced by force, fraud or coercion, or in which the person induced to perform such an act has not attained eighteen years of age. Basically speaking, anytime someone is under eighteen years of age and is performing any commercial sex act, it is by law human trafficking. Force, fraud or coercion is not necessary to make it illegal.

- War children—these are children who are often stolen from their homes and forced to fight in tribal wars. This practice is mainly found in African countries such as Uganda, Ghana and the Democratic Republic of Congo.

"Modern-day slavery," by contrast, is when an individual or group completely controls another individual or group, often using violence, for economic gain. Although there are slight distinctions between these terms, they are often used interchangeably.

In modern times international trading has become more accessible not only to legitimate global enterprises but also to criminals. Free markets enable us to own products from all over the world at affordable prices. Criminals have applied this same logic to the trading and selling of human beings. Two hundred years ago, when slavery was legal, slaves were seen as an investment; the average price for an African slave was $40,000. Today the average cost of a slave is $90. Slaves today are considered a disposable commodity.[5]

As I've wrestled with this issue I've often wondered, what can I do? I'm not a staffer at the United Nations or member of the State Department. I have no direct line to an embassy anywhere in the world where I can share my concerns. I might watch, read and pray, but then, more often than not, I simply move on with the day and leave whatever story, person or tragedy I've discovered on the computer screen, the memory filed somewhere under "deal with later" or "can't deal with at all."

How do we interact with slavery in our towns, with our children, in our communities and churches? If we're honest, we often submit to a pervasive mindset toward evil: as long as it's distant from us, we accept it. We know that prostitution exists, for example, but we've never noticed a brothel next to our local Target. Our hearts go out to those wounded girls who have no parents to love them, but we assume they're there for reasons that have nothing to do with us. Didn't they choose that lifestyle? Aren't they in it for drugs? Rebellion? When we do see prostitution up close—say, in Las Vegas or Amsterdam, where it's legal and regulated—we don't see slaves. These are businesswomen. We've been programmed to believe prostitution is a victimless crime.

The Frederick Douglass Family Foundation describes sexual slavery as "a crime hiding beneath what is perceived as a lesser crime."

Prostitution gains a kind of legendary or honored status because it is oft-handedly called the oldest profession. But look closer at the larger portion of the sex industry and you'll find that it could be more accurately called the oldest form of slavery with a long history of women and children being forced to pleasure men in order to enrich their masters.[6]

We simply have not heard the stories of how these women came to sell their bodies. Who gets the money? Why do they stay? It is a great lie of all of history that prostitution is primarily due to the sin and free will of a woman.

Sex slavery is the most lucrative form of modern-day slavery, but slavery takes many other forms today:

- *Chattel slavery* is the most similar to the African slave trade of history. People are sold and bought—they become property and they can be treated however their owner decides.

- *Debt bondage* is similar to the indentured servanthood we learned about in textbooks, holding its victims in an endless cycle of debt. Over two billion people live on less than a dollar a day. This extreme poverty pushes parents to offer their children as "workers" to pay off a debt. Parents are told the child will work only until the debt is paid, but the criminals inflate interest rates, lie and exploit. There are cases in Nepal and India where generations after generations of families have worked as slaves, all beginning with a small loan from a great-grandparent.

- *Forced labor* is a form of slavery where victims are lured by the promise of a good job. Upon arriving at the farm, plantation or mine, they find themselves in slave conditions. No pay, physical and mental abuse, and no freedom to leave.

- *Child soldiers* are children taken from their homes and forced to fight for a militia group. This horrific type of forced labor is found in parts of Central Africa, such as the Democratic Republic of the Congo, and parts of Southeast Asia.

The question remains, "What does this have to do with us?" The reality is that slavery touches real aspects of our lives. From the minerals mined to manufacture our mobile phones, to the harvested chocolate we feed our children, to the sex trade surrounding major sporting events in our own backyards, slavery is part of our lives.

Here are some common areas in which trafficking victims have been identified in the United States:

- *The commercial sex industry.* Domestic street prostitution; strip clubs; escort agencies; massage parlors; residential brothels; "hostess" clubs; residential or underground brothels; cantina bars; and any prostitution controlled by pimps, whether hotel-based, street-based, Internet-based, escort-based, truck stop-based or via online websites such as Craigslist or Backpage.

- *Agriculture.* Unsafe working conditions, slave-wages, exploitative labor practices.

- *Industry and manufacturing.* Factories, construction, large factory work.

- *Retail businesses.* Restaurants, nail salons, hair-braiding salons, magazine-sales crews, flower- and candy-sales crews.

- *Private homes.* Domestic servitude, bride trafficking, maids and housekeepers.

As I have woken up to these realities, I've become inspired by my abolitionist sisters of two hundred years ago. It's been pointed out by historians that in both England and the United States, during the nineteenth-century abolitionist movement, women could not vote, were not public speakers or teachers, held no political office and could not be clergy. And yet women played a central role in bringing an end to the trans-Atlantic slave trade. In societies where ordinary women seemed to have little influence, they became the backbone of a movement that changed history. As author Adam Hochschild explains,

> The women's societies were almost always bolder than those of men. . . . Men recognized that it was the women who were keeping the movement alive at a difficult time. "Ladies' Associations did everything," a prominent male activist acknowledged. "They circulated publications: they procured money to publish; they dunned and talked and coaxed and lectured; they got up in public meetings and filled our halls and platforms when the day arrived; they carried round petitions and enforced the duty of signing them. . . . In a word they formed the cement of the whole antislavery building."[7]

Two hundred years ago slavery was legal. If someone worked on a slave ship or, even better, captained a slave ship, he was considered to have achieved economic and career success. Somehow society did not consider it a crime to kidnap, chain, rape and sell another human being. In fact, slave merchants were proud of themselves for developing such a lucrative global business. Internationally many men became very rich buying and selling slaves.

It was Christian women, both in England and in the United States, who started to speak out that they believed slavery to be a sin. Despite the prevalent belief that slave labor was essential to the Western economy, devoted women worked tirelessly for decades in the abolitionist movement, believing they had a moral and religious duty.

The abolitionist movement was a messy business back then—and extremely radical. Very few activists agreed on the best strategies. There were many different expressions of abolitionism, and the movement was almost snuffed out many times. It was women who remained tenacious in their belief, despite the radical global change they were seeking, that their cause was just, true and right and therefore would triumph.

Women's involvement in abolitionist activities was complicated by the parallel fight for women's rights. Many good Christian women were worried about the propriety of being involved in abolitionist meetings, groups and activities. This was a real barrier for the growth of the movement. But the very nature of what was needed to build the movement expanded the role of women in society, in the economy and in politics. Over time their strong conviction that slavery was wrong pushed women to participate in things they never would have before.

Another barrier for the growth of the abolitionist movement was the role of churches. Many pastors believed that to immediately free all slaves and to end the slave trade would be devastating to the Western world's economy and was simply not realistic. Many women gave up expecting their church leaders to take a strong lead in the cause against slavery and accused them of supporting slavery by their apathy and inaction.

During this time it was Quaker and evangelical middle-class women (many of whom lived on rural farms) who worked tirelessly to raise awareness. In her book *The Great Silent Army of Abolitionism: Ordinary Women in the Antislavery Movement*, Julie Roy Jeffrey tells story after story of women who felt pulled by the demands of their everyday lives, caring for their homes and children, and were unsure how they would find the time and strength to participate in the movement. Yet history shows they did find the time and began to organize themselves.

Women formed antislavery societies similar to contemporary Bible studies or book clubs. Jeffrey explains, "Antislavery societies offered women more than the opportunity to support emancipation. They created opportunities for friendship, conviviality, and emotional support and a worthwhile pastime outside of the home."[8] What is so remarkable is that this was the first time in history a mass movement of ordinary citizens rose up and fought for the rights of a group of people who had no family, tribal or national connection to them. (For example, English Quaker women mobilized on behalf of slave laborers on plantations in the Caribbean—a place and a people far removed from them.) Today when we organize ourselves and mobilize others to fight crimes against humanity, we are taking our cues from the activities of these ordinary citizens. There are many similarities in what we do today as "activists" to this period of history and the abolitionists of two hundred years ago.

What did these women do, and how can we fight modern-day slavery in the same spirit and with the same tenacity?

- *They prayed.* Women were motivated by their faith and their strong conviction that slavery was evil. They met and prayed for wisdom, guidance and the end of slavery in their world. They prayed with belief that slavery could be defeated.

- *They formed sewing circles.* Women gathered in small groups in their homes and sewed together. They made garments for both former slaves and those still enslaved. They made things to sell to raise money for the cause. Most important, they found each other—like-minded women gathered for conversation, education and mutual support.

- *They created and organized fairs.* Think bake sale, garage sale, craft show. Women put on abolitionist fairs for decades between 1820 and 1850. At the fairs these women would raise awareness and money, circulating petitions for signatures, setting up lectures and providing goods to be sold.

- *They spread the word.* At a time when women were expected to be active only in the home, when women held no political or clerical office, they began writing, traveling and speaking in front of large audiences to raise awareness. Newspapers such as *The Freedom Herald, The Liberator, The Philanthropist* and *The Anti-Slavery Almanac* consistently published articles and poems written by women. Women circulated the abolitionist newspapers by giving them to friends, buying extra copies and handing them out to neighbors. They passed out tracts, papers, documents—anything that publicized the views of the anti-slavery movement.

- *They boycotted products produced by slaves.* Women abolitionists in the 1800s identified slave-free products and urged their families and communities to buy them. Historian Adam Hochschild tells the story of an English woman named Elizabeth Heyrick, a former schoolteacher and a Quaker who began a sugar boycott in her hometown. She visited all the grocers, urging them not to stock slave-grown goods. She was smart and feisty, and she was fed up with a government and a system that was doing nothing about slavery. "The West Indian planter and the people of this country stand in the same moral relations to each other, as the thief and the receiver of stolen goods. . . . Why petition Parliament at all? To do that for us, which we can do more speedily and more effectually for ourselves?"[9] Heyrick understood that companies and governments would respond if the consumer stopped buying and demanded change. This act of boycotting a product was the first of its kind and is believed to have tipped the scales in the fight to end the African slave trade.

As modern-day abolitionists, we have all these things at our disposal and more. Our gatherings may look a little different. We may be chatting on a Facebook group page instead of in a sewing circle in a quiet living room lit by candlelight. We may be circulating websites, articles and information about organizations across our computer screens instead of circulating print newspapers. We may meet together at the local wine and cheese shop rather than at the meeting hall. But the spirit of our abolitionist sisters lives on.

Today, many individuals have become rich buying and selling slaves. But today women are beginning to organize themselves to fight. The slavery of our generation is not a legal, culturally acceptable, open activity as it was during the time of the African slave trade. It is insidious. It is difficult to define, keep track of, prosecute and end. Those who engage in the trafficking of other humans have a well-run underground machine that moves people unseen and undetected all over the world.

But we can gain strength from the spirit and example of those women of the 1800s who believed that their cause was true and that they had a responsibility to not give up. We can match their tenacity and not allow ourselves to be overwhelmed or paralyzed by the magnitude of the problem. Like them, we can refuse to nothing. We can organize. We can educate and put pressure on companies to produce only slave-free products. We must have no tolerance for even one man, woman or child being held against his or her will in our world.

Like the criminals who traffic in human beings, we too are an elusive power—a power that doesn't organize underground but rather around kitchen tables, at soccer fields, in Bible studies and in carpool lanes. Together we create the solution. Together we must begin.

Reflect

1. Does the thought of becoming an abolitionist overwhelm you?
   Excite you? Discourage you? Why?

2. What are the barriers you face in joining the fight to end modern-
   day slavery?

Take Action

Pray. In researching this book we interviewed people from everyday
moms to those on the front lines in Cambodia to world leaders. We
asked them, "What would you tell the everyday American she can
do to fight modern-day slavery?" Unanimously we were told, "Pray."

3

I'm a Soccer Mom, Not an Activist

Kimberly McOwen Yim

Every great dream begins with a dreamer.
Always remember, you have within you the strength, the patience,
and the passion to reach for the stars to change the world.

HARRIET TUBMAN

In 2007 I started working part-time with my father, helping him start a charitable arm of his company. Some of my responsibilities were administrative, some a bit of research, and still more relationship-building with many of the nonprofit organizations the company supported. I enjoy my job tremendously; I find the work interesting and enjoy the time I get to spend with my father.

The job has opened up opportunities for me to learn about what's going on in other parts of the world. Three years ago we were invited by a guy we were doing business with to attend a film screening. All we knew was that it was about human trafficking, but at the time neither of us knew what that term meant. I think our main motivation for attending was to support this new colleague who was also becoming a friend.

I chuckled as I entered the theater, keenly aware that we were some of the oldest people in the room. The room was full of college-aged hipsters. I wished I had grabbed my trucker hat and scarf as accessories.

The film, *Call + Response*, is a hip rockumentary directed and produced by musician-turned-activist Justin Dillon. Throughout the film big-name politicians and journalists share stories about what's going on in our world. Famous actresses and leaders in the new abo-

Kimberly with Justin Dillon, director and producer of *Call + Response*

litionist movement are interviewed about what they're doing to combat the growing and incredibly profitable slavery industry.

Between the interviews, trendy musicians play powerful songs, some written to offer a voice to those trapped in slavery, some written to inspire the listener to action. An extremely powerful aspect of the film is the link made between music and slavery. The colorful, intensely brilliant and sometimes radical Cornel West masterfully paints a picture of slaves of the early nineteenth century, singing spirituals in the call-and-response fashion. West shows how this foundational style shapes what we love about music today.

Toward the end of *Call + Response* Dillon poses a question that still haunts me: "What will your response be?" The film ends with "Be the response."

When the film was over I could barely lift my head. My eyes fought back tears. I was surprised by what I had seen and the effect it had had on me.

With my heart burning I made my way to the front to greet Justin Dillon and to thank him for his powerful film. I also thanked our friend profusely for the invitation, embarrassed that I had totally underestimated what I was going to see that evening.

My dad and I walked silently to the car. We were both aware that something significant had happened in that room—the weight very real on both our hearts, the ramifications yet unknown. I had always considered slavery to be in the past—long-ago history. *Call + Response* jolted me awake to the reality slavery is here and now.

If slavery exists now, that means there are slaves now. Real people—children, women and men—brutally forced to work for the benefit of others. Not free to live their life. Some are literally chained in cages, others locked behind the gates of million-dollar homes. Some appear to live freely among us.

Some modern-day slaves are migrant workers tricked to work in tomato fields without pay. Others are ten-year-old girls in Thailand, forced to smile while offering sexual services to foreign men. Others are generational brick workers in India who know nothing but the four walls of the factory they grew up in and can never leave. There are very young boys who are given AK-47s and forced to rape and kill for their survival in the mining areas of Eastern Congo. There are local victims—those in our own backyards, such as the at-risk youth in the United States being moved from one professional sporting event to another in order to appease the sexual appetite of men who attend these games.

All these real people have very different circumstances. Their living conditions, race, age and nationality vary, yet each one is enslaved. They cannot walk away from their situations because of force, the threat of violence, coercion or fraud.

The days following the screening I couldn't shake what I'd learned. My frustration grew as my questions remained unanswered. I knew I was at a crossroads. I could turn and walk away, or I could face it and lean into this crisis.

I remember the day I sat at my computer and began my search for answers. I had chosen to lean in.

I thought I would experience some peace after I found some answers, but my frustration only grew. I became angry as I learned more. Most of the information I found was old news—more than five years old. People had been fighting hard on behalf of victims of these atrocious crimes for over a decade, and I was just now hearing about it?

Why aren't we talking about it? I screamed to myself.

The "we" I was referring to was me, my friends, the media, my family—everyone. Why do we know more about Paris Hilton than we know about slavery? Why is our media more focused on which celebrity is in what rehab center or wearing which fashion designer to an awards show?

I attempted, rather pathetically, to talk about slavery with those in my circle of influence—friends, family and neighbors. I quickly became a buzz kill. When is the appropriate time to talk about slavery? How does it come up in casual conversation? I tried to share what I was learning and got only blank, glazed looks in return. I interpreted these as "You're crazy."

Call + Response eventually came out in a theater about thirty miles from where I live. I recruited one of my favorite people—my sister—to go see it with me. She was cautiously open to it; I think she attended mostly to support me, as she could tell I was bursting at the seams with passion.

Having someone to talk to about the film helped relieve the pressure boiling in my gut, and I began to sense I needed to do more. How was I to be the response? How would I respond to what I now knew?

I brought these questions to the Lord. I wrestled with them as I continued to research modern-day slavery. I signed up to receive updates from organizations on the front lines of the fight, such as International Justice Mission and Free the Slaves. I began to read books.

Yet I experienced some conflict. Like everyone, I'm human. I doubt myself and God all the time. How could I—a wife, a mother of two, a part-time worker, a resident of Orange County—put a dent in this problem? I'm a soccer mom, not an activist.

But instinctively I knew I had to start somewhere.

A First Step

Making my way to my seat at Not For Sale's Global Forum on Human Trafficking, I started to notice a pattern. Once again I was one of the oldest people in the room and maybe the only mom. Okay, there were a few, but anyone who looked older than thirty was working at a booth for a nonprofit organization or volunteering for the church that helped host the event. Although I was happy to see so many young people passionately engaged in fighting modern-day slavery, I still could not find my place in this new abolitionist movement. I was inspired and learned much that day, but what I took away most was the deep understanding that more people in my demographic needed to be engaged.

And yet I still felt an intense inner conflict. The people I was reading about were on the front lines, working for organizations and making a difference: rescuing, advocating for or restoring

those victimized by slavery. Any organization I researched that provided training or offered internships targeted college-age students.
As a mother, I had to keep rolling on in the day-to-day as if all was
great in the world. I couldn't leave my kids for three weeks to be
trained in Northern California. I couldn't go to Cambodia and
rescue young girls from the sex trade. I love being a mother more
than anything in the world, but it seemed there was nothing I
could do that would make any kind of impact in helping eradicate
slavery as long as I was in the mommy season of my life. The
problem was too big.

I felt like a hypocrite. What God was doing inside me was not
matching my external reality. My heart ached and I was paralyzed.
Many mornings after taking my kids to school I would walk the
beach trail, sunglasses fogged, as I tried to hold back tears of sorrow
rolling down my cheeks. Images of six-year-old girls offering sexual
services cut my soul. I would often find myself sitting in the sand
crying in sorrow and rage, "Lord, what can I do?"

I come from a Christian faith tradition that believes God can use
you right where you are, in any situation. My situation was motherhood, and despite what I had been taught and believed, I wasn't
sure God was going to use me in the fight against slavery. I began
to wish that I were still in college. I would major in criminal justice
and really make an impact. Or if only I could win the lottery—I
would provide a new shelter and fund new anti-trafficking efforts.

It took some time for me to understand that what the movement
really needed was more everyday people. Regular moms, dads,
grandparents, teachers, nurses, dentists, accountants, professors,
business owners, senior citizens, physical therapists, doctors, jan-
itors, bartenders, artists—anyone without a fancy title or who
thought they didn't have any power. There were already super-
heroes in the new abolitionist movement—people who had
rescued enslaved families, fought tirelessly for pieces of legislation

to make all kinds of slavery illegal once and for all, and rearranged their lives to care for, love and restore the lives of trafficking victims. What was missing in the new abolitionist movement was people like me.

What was missing was people like you.

Reflect

1. Does this chapter create any big ideas about how you can engage others and make a difference? What are they?

2. Do you doubt yourself and your ability to make a difference and raise awareness? If so, why? Where do you think those messages are coming from? How can you overcome them?

Take Action

Watch the film *Call + Response* with a friend or two. Check in with each other a week later on your reaction to the challenge to "be the response."

4

Abolitionist Mamas

Kimberly McOwen Yim

*Jesus invites us to accept his burden, which is
the burden of the whole world, a burden that includes human
suffering in all times and all places. But this divine burden is light,
and we carry it when our heart has been transformed into
the gentle and humble heart of our Lord.*

HENRI NOUWEN, *THE WAY OF THE HEART*

After months of reading books and articles on the subject of slavery, I became sick of it. It was starting to feel like just another hobby. I could no longer simply sit behind my computer signing up for every anti-trafficking organization's email updates; I had to act. I had to move. I had to share what I was learning with the people I knew.

I could picture it: an anti-trafficking movie screening at my church, packed full of the citizens of San Clemente. Community leaders, the press and other notables in attendance. My hometown becoming known not only for its great surf but also for great compassion. San Clemente: the first modern-day abolitionist city.

But then I hit the brakes. I couldn't even get anyone to engage in a conversation about the subject of slavery. How would I get people to come to a church and see a film about a totally depressing topic?

I switched the plan to something more doable. How could I get people to my house to see the film? In the past I had hosted clothing, jewelry and scrapbooking parties; why not have a house party of sorts? Once I put my idea in the context of what I had done before, it seemed pos-

sible. I still wasn't confident people would come, but the heaviness I was carrying was starting to lighten as I began to act on my convictions where I felt the Lord was leading.

Who would come to a party to learn about modern-day slavery? I sent an Evite to about forty women I knew in my community, inviting them to my home to watch the International Justice Mission documentary *At the*

Kimberly and Shayne at the Global Forum on Human Trafficking, San Francisco

End of Slavery. I mentioned that wine and dessert would be served—my attempt to counteract the heaviness of the topic. I put a packet of information together people could take home as a resource and then waited for the RSVPs to come in.

Fourteen women attended my first event, each of them curious and thankful for the invitation. One friend said something that so deeply connected with my own journey that it has informed everything I do in my fight against slavery since: "Kim, I will join you as long as you tell me what I can do about it. I don't want to come and be involved unless you tell me what I can do to make the situation better."

That, apparently, is a common sentiment. At the end of the evening two of my guests gave me huge hugs and said, "You tell us what to do next and we will." I was deeply grateful for their support, and without thinking I blurted out my dream for a "big city event." That night I went to bed encouraged, and the next morning I began to plan how to get the whole city involved.

Needless to say, the next few months were rough. It took me a while to learn: dream big, start small.

Over a year after first seeing *Call + Response*, I finally got my hands on a copy of the film. It hadn't been officially released to DVD yet, so there were conditions—one of them being that I could use it only in my home. With my grand plan of a large city event in mind, I spent weeks soliciting local business owners to come to my house and see the film. Again I enticed people with the promise of wine and dessert.

Looking back, I can see it may have been a little naïve to walk into a surf shop and introduce myself: "Hi. I'm a local mother of two kids. I want to show you this film on slavery that changed my life. I think it will resonate with you and the entire surf community." I eventually had three home screenings of the film; three local business owners, two local youth pastors and a childhood friend attended.

Everyone thought the film was great, yet only one woman truly caught my big vision. Dawn, a mother and owner of The Cellar—a hip, industrial-rustic wine and cheese bar—became not only a trusted friend but also, through her restaurant, the catalyst for much of what my new abolitionist friends would do.

Becoming "We"

It took me a few weeks to get a plan to move forward underway. The peace I felt having found a like-minded woman in Dawn began to wane the more time that passed by. I knew I needed more people to catch the vision, but I had exhausted all my ideas. Feelings of defeat began to creep in again.

I love Wednesday nights. I take my kids to the midweek program at church, and I walk to a local restaurant with my friend Allison to grab a happy hour dinner—sirloin steak or some salmon and a glass of pinot grigio.

One Wednesday night I was feeling particularly emotional over all my efforts at trying to get people engaged. I couldn't see that I was making any impact. I sat with tears streaming down my face. Like a good girlfriend, Allison listened, and then she gave me some thoughtful advice.

"Why don't you invite those fourteen women that came to your first event? They seemed to be interested, and a couple of them seem to be ready to do something."

Friends are such game-changers. *Genius!* was my thought as I ended my tearfest and ordered a coffee.

I went back to my original list of invitees and had one more house party showing the film that impacted me so deeply. That night three more extraordinary women emerged: Lisa, Tracy and Julie. God had now brought together five of us who were committed to raising awareness about modern-day slavery. My lonely "I" became a "we" and it made all the difference. We were abolitionists.

The five of us began meeting to talk about the best way to go about reaching our community. With all of us mothers, and a couple of us working other jobs outside the home, we acknowledged our limited time and resources. Yet I still had this grandiose idea of a city event where thousands would come, their lives would be changed and everyone would be inspired to change the world!

A more realistic first step began to form. We wanted to reach as many people as we could in our immediate spheres of influence first. We knew we didn't want to become an official organization.

We agreed we needed to stay grassroots because that's what was feasible, what we could commit to within the limits of our circumstances. Our goal was simply to educate and inspire others in our community to engage the issue, to provide practical ways any person could get involved—regardless of season of life—in reabolishing slavery.

We gathered at Dawn's wine and cheese bar. The Cellar, with its dimly lit interior, wood beams and floors, and polished-concrete bar, was a nice escape from peanut butter sandwiches and the taxicab driving existence most of us were living. Since as both mom and restaurant owner Dawn was the busiest of us all, The Cellar became a convenient and fun spot to meet. The wine and cheese we sampled during our meetings made our gathering social as well as meaningful. We enjoyed the friendly camaraderie of getting to know each other.

As we continued to plan we came to eventually see that The Cellar was evolving into more than a fun place to meet. It was becoming a sacred space where our common desire for justice met our individual skills. After and before our events we prayed, ate and toasted. Specialized cheeses and signature drinks became a staple, celebrating our being together and at the same time symbolizing our solidarity with the women—some literally halfway around the world—we hoped we were supporting.

I was trying to get organized. I made large orange postcards to pass out to people interested in learning what they could do about human trafficking. On one side of the postcard I listed general facts and statistics; on the other side I listed ten action items. I named the print document "Abolitionist Mama."

At the time I thought the title was simply a means of finding my project later on Vista Print's home page. I didn't know until the postcards arrived in the mail that the title would be printed in the corner of the each card. This second-thought title became incredibly meaningful. It stuck. Our little band of world changers began to call ourselves Abolitionist Mamas.

As Abolitionist Mamas we were determined to become more than people who agreed that slavery was wrong. We wanted to become women who actively worked to right a wrong. Millions of slaves in our world was not okay with us. We could not sit in our comfortable houses and simply say, "That's really sad." As my friend Tracy declared at the end of one of our meetings, "Feeling sad is not enough!" We wanted to become part of the solution and we wanted what we knew to be true to match how we lived. We wanted to be examples to our children of what compassionate people do and how compassionate people live. Tracy said vehemently, "I hope my children will learn compassion through my efforts and continue to rage on for justice."

As Abolitionist Mamas we represent three different churches and one Jewish center. We saw the similarities and differences of our faith backgrounds as an asset to reaching out to our community. We were committed to be a community endeavor and not a specific church effort.

My big city dream eventually came true. Abolitionist Mamas hosted a VIP event to screen *Call + Response*. Close friends and family were invited, as well as those in positions of influence in our community—pastors, youth pastors, city council members, business owners, teachers, musicians and principals. We pooled personal funds and received some generous donations in order to rent the historic Casino of San Clemente, a newly renovated building in town. We even flew in Justin Dillon, producer of the film that got the whole ball rolling, for a question-and-answer session after the screening. We were thoughtful and strategic as we wanted our guests to be inspired to act on what they would learn.

Bubbling with anticipation and dressed in *Call + Response* white T-shirts, we ran around completing some final details. Twinkling lights and candles lined the brick courtyard leading to the Casino, where over a hundred guests joined us for our event. Within the courtyard a large fireplace blazed. Cocktail tables were draped with burlap tablecloths and decorated with succulent arrangements and tea lights. We mingled with guests as appetizers by some of our favorite local eateries were served. Finally everyone filed into the rustic saloon to view the film.

The San Clemente Abolitionist Mamas

For so long I had felt alone. Now I was tremendously empowered because I had found like-minded friends. I quickly learned that our different talents and abilities would make whatever we did much better, more professional and a lot more fun because we would do it together. As Tracy said, "I know I can use my voice, but when I joined my voice with others I knew someone would hear."

Reflect

1. Why are you reading this book? Have you felt alone and over-whelmed by the issue of modern-day slavery?

2. Which issues discussed in this chapter make your heart burn? Which inspire you?

Take Action

1. Host a screening of *Call + Response* in your community (call andresponse.com).

2. Identify and reach out to friends who can join you on the journey toward becoming a modern-day abolitionist. Begin meeting regularly with them. Get educated and mobilized to act together.

5

Excuses

Kimberly McOwen Yim
and Shayne Moore

*The truth does not change according
to our ability to stomach it.*

FLANNERY O'CONNOR

When God first broke our hearts and woke us up to the harsh reality of modern-day slavery, we were distraught. We were both informed women who understood that injustices were a part of our world. We had experienced pain and heartbreak in our own lives. Yet the existence of the brutalities of slavery in our time was a weight we could not shake. This heartbreak changed the trajectory of our lives. It rearranged our schedules and it woke us in the middle of the night. It forced us on our knees in desperate weeping to our Lord for direction.

But as we were overwhelmed by the magnitude of the issue, the sadness sunk in and we entered into a season of being stuck. We felt trapped by inaction—in our duties and the responsibilities we had to our families, jobs and communities.

At first we came up with an abundance of excuses. We didn't have time to do anything about the heartbreak. That's what the church was for. We needed better leaders in our world. We already had enough responsibilities in our lives. We could not possibly take on something else. Modern-day slavery was just too difficult and too complicated—and, to be honest, simply too traumatizing to hear about. Besides, who were we to make a difference?

Because God is a God of grace, he met us in our stuckness. As we sat ashamed of our inaction and feelings of inadequacy, in the midst of our quiet moments of fear and dread for our world and the realities of real people caught in horrific conditions, God spoke to our depths and reminded us that he is with the brokenhearted. We allowed our hearts to be broken by the things that break the heart of God.

And slavery shattered our hearts.

We pressed on. We read more books, we blogged and we talked things over with friends. We planned educational events and attended conferences. We found like-minded women, discovered soul sisters and began to see God present in this catastrophic evil in our world. The anger and grief stopped being the loudest voice, and hope began to emerge.

Tears of anguish for those suffering were replaced with a strong belief that God would act. He has not forgotten those held against their will for evil purposes and gains of others. In the spirit of Isaiah 58, we desired to spend ourselves on behalf of the poor and oppressed. We didn't know exactly what this would look like or what God would require of us. And setting aside our own fears and excuses was a challenge. But we had wrestled with God and put our foot in the ring. We were in this fight. We were abolitionists—even if we were starting as timid fighters in the corner.

◆ ◆ ◆

Shayne had just returned from speaking at a Women Who Stand event put on by World Relief. She called filled with good news:

"Kim!" she said as soon as I answered. "This amazing group of women has invited us to travel to Cambodia and learn what World Relief is doing to fight slavery!"

World Relief is an organization whose purpose is to stand with the most vulnerable in the world. They work to empower local churches in the United States and around the world so they can better serve the vulnerable in their own communities. They have initiatives in education, health, child development, agriculture, anti-trafficking, disaster relief, refugee resettlement, food security and microenterprise. World Relief has had a strong presence in Cambodia for more than ten years, and a group of women from the Baltimore area was going to learn more about the work there. They wanted Shayne and me to join them.

Shayne continued, excited, "I've always wanted to go to Cambodia! To see it all firsthand would be an irreplaceable experience."

Shayne prattled on about the details. I listened but dismissed her. I knew I wasn't going.

Cambodia was just too far away. Besides, I'd been telling people how much there was to do right in our own homes to fight slavery without having to go overseas. I couldn't see any reason why I would go. I put the request in the back of my mind and thought if I ignored it the idea of this crazy trip would be a fleeting moment.

A week later Shayne called me. "Kim," she said. "Have you made a decision about the Cambodia trip?"

Apparently her idea didn't float away. Shayne was still enthusiastic and felt pulled to Cambodia. She was impressed with World Relief and she wanted to touch, feel, smell and hug the Cambodian people. Having already traveled to other parts of the world to learn what life was like for other mothers and children who were struggling in poverty, she was determined to see in person exactly what was happening in Cambodia—the notorious place where sex trafficking and sex tourism go unchecked.

I moaned out loud and confessed to her that I hadn't thought about it much and still needed to talk it over with my husband. I was thankful we lived across the country from one another so she couldn't see my dismissive expression. I had no intention of going. I had stubbornly refused to pray, talk it over with my husband or think over the logistics of what I would do with my kids.

But I knew this request would not go away by my simply ignoring it. I needed to give Shayne a definitive answer, as I knew there were other women holding a spot for us on this trip.

At some point I did eventually pray about it, but my prayers went like this: "Lord, I don't want to go. I don't think you want me to go, so you can find something else that will stand in the way of my going—maybe an opportunity in Washington, D.C. That's a place I would actually like to visit and could bring my kids. That would be great. Amen."

There was a heaviness on my heart as I tried to find a good time to talk about the trip with my husband. Cambodia was an area of the world I had never had a desire to visit. It was far away—like around the world far—and I knew it could not be a long weekend type of trip. If I went I would be gone for more than a week. That thought alone made me miss my kids.

Yet I was conflicted, refusing to admit a tug to go. Driving around town doing errands in the quiet of my car, I would find myself tearing up. It became clear that my only hope in not going was my husband. John could always be relied on to offer common sense. I was sure he would not like this idea. It would put an immense strain on him for me to be gone so long. It wouldn't work. He would remind me. John would be my out.

After the kids were asleep, I told John about the opportunity to go to Cambodia.

I poured out the details of the trip, quickly reminding him that Cambodia was really far away. I'd be on the other side of the world. I understood that it would be too difficult for him and the kids.

There. I could tell Shayne I had talked to John. I was happy to have this chore out of the way and was on my way to do the dishes when John said, "I agree with Shayne. You should go."

"What?" I whispered in shock.

The tears I had been holding back began to roll down my face, surprising him.

"Why are you so apprehensive about going?" he asked.

"It's so far. So far from you and the kids," I stammered and sniffled.

"Oh, we'll be fine," John assured me. "You have to go. You have to see these realities. You have to tell these stories." I let out a long sigh and turned back to do the dishes.

I was going to Cambodia.

Occasionally I would tear up just thinking about going. When sharing prayer requests with my small group, I could barely say two words before I broke down like a baby and cried. We had been meeting for ten years and I had never broken down and sobbed. It was becoming embarrassing. I hadn't even bought my plane ticket and I was having a physical reaction to missing my kids.

I was about to leave for Cambodia when circumstances conspired to increase my anxiety even more. My husband injured his back, my eight-year-old son broke his tibia and—unbelievably—Shayne was not going. She needed a full hip-replacement surgery ASAP as her arthritis had advanced to the point that she could barely walk. During this time I reached out to my sister and my closest friends asking them to pray for me.

A journal-keeper since high school, I've found over the years that my prayer journal is a safe place to pour out all my off-the-wall, overemotional, passionate and often redundant prayers, pleas and thanksgivings to the Lord. As my life became full of kids and family responsibilities, the habit waned, but I did continue to grab my journal in crisis moments or when I was full of ideas.

This was one of those times. So I turned to the Lord and in writing to him found some clarity. I slowly began to see what I had already known: that when God calls us to a project, to a change of lifestyle—to anything, really—he may not clear our paths to help us get there easily. Imagine that. In slowing down and writing down my fears and concerns to the Lord, I began to understand that obstacles are not always God's way of redirecting us. Sometimes the obstacles are there to prepare us for the journey, the path he is calling us to take.

Here I was talking regularly about ways for everyday, ordinary women to engage in the issue of human trafficking, and I was taken off guard when presented with an unexpected turn of events. Writing down my fears and handing them over to the Lord through the ink of my pen, I began to see that this is life—challenges, obstacles and pain are to be expected. As a believer I do not need to fear or frantically fight change or challenges. For I have hope: not the empty hope of wishful thinking or positive energy, but the hope of the resurrected Christ.

In 2 Corinthians 12, Paul boasts of his sufferings. In the past I'd found this passage kind of odd, but during this time of fearful excuse-making I began to see what Paul was saying with greater clarity. With earnest pleading and genuine love for the people, Paul explains that the many sufferings he faced in obedience to the Lord's calling were to keep him humble and to let them know he gained nothing in pleading with them to follow the Lord Jesus Christ. In fact, the only thing he gained in doing so was more suffering. He now boasts of his suffering as a way to remind the Corinthians that the only reason he continually reaches out to them is out of obedience to the Lord Jesus Christ and his love for them.

The part that particularly struck me was Paul's explanation of how three times he pleaded with the Lord to take away his suffering, but the Lord replied, "My grace is sufficient for you, for my power is made perfect in weakness" (2 Corinthians 12:9). The lesson Paul has learned, he shares. "Therefore I will boast all the more gladly about my weaknesses, so that Christ's power may rest on me. That is why, for Christ's sake, I delight in weakness, in insults, in hardships, in persecutions, in difficulties. For when I am weak, then I am strong" (2 Corinthians 12:9-10).

Although I had asked my friends to pray for clarity on this Cambodia trip, the clarity I received was this: In my weakness I am strong. God's power—his will—is made perfect in my weakness. I can delight in the Lord as his power rests on me in hardships and in the difficulties I will face. This didn't necessarily answer all of my questions directly, but it did give me great peace that I would be okay without Shayne in Cambodia.

I continued planning to go to Cambodia, but I also knew that if anything changed, I would adapt. Learning to expect challenges is a lesson I have had to learn time and time again in life, and it is no different when we step out and join God in exposing the injustices of the world. Trusting the Lord when I feel empowered and strong is easy, but trusting when I feel weak and when I step into the uncomfortable territory of the unknown is terribly difficult, and my excuses are exposed.

When I left for Cambodia, my son's leg was still broken and Shayne was having surgery. But I met women from around the world who taught me firsthand about the rescue and rehabilitation of trafficked victims in this unfamiliar country. In my weakness, he was strong. Some excuses are just not good excuses.

Reflect

1. What are you afraid of?

Take Action

1. Do you have anxieties about how to get involved? If so, meet with trusted friends and family. Ask them to pray for you.

Thick Skin and Tender Hearts

Kimberly McOwen Yim
and Shayne Moore

> *The last people who should get caught off guard by*
> *injustice in the world should be Bible-believing Christians.*

GARY HAUGEN,
INTERNATIONAL JUSTICE MISSION

When we have spoken about modern-day slavery, women have often stopped us midsentence, saying, "I can't hear it! It's just too much!"

So we stop. We bite our tongues, but inside we're screaming, "Are you kidding me? There are thousands and thousands women, girls and boys trapped, often beaten and raped night after night for the profit of their slaveholder, and you, in the comfort of this coffeehouse sipping your latté, can't hear it?"

Instead of sharing our thoughts, we take a deep breath and remind ourselves that what we're trying to share with friends and family is disturbing. It may be the most unpleasant thing they've heard in a long time. They may have daughters of their own, or a granddaughter, and this may hit too close to home.

Hearing about the business of sex trafficking is beyond uncomfortable. For us it is the most difficult topic within the global issue of human trafficking with which to engage. Our daughters were little when we first woke up to what was going on regarding the exploitation of human beings. We lost sleep after reading about how four-, five- and six-year-olds were forced to smile when they offered oral sex to customers, waiting for the day their virginity would be sold once the price was high enough. How do mothers, fathers, decent human beings go on living their comfortable lives once they know about the horrors others endure every day?

Living as we do in the midst of the comforts of our sanitized society it can be difficult to imagine the nightmare of others' lives. It's a challenge to think that there's any good purpose to knowing about the tragedies of slavery since it seems there is nothing we can do to alleviate the situation. The problems of this world just seem too big and too far away.

So we turn up our stereos, we turn on our "reality" TV and press through life. Happiness for ourselves and our families becomes our goal. If bad news can't be relieved by the baking of a casserole or a note of encouragement, we just don't want to hear it. We quote Scripture like Romans 8:28, telling people "that in all things God works for the good of those who love him." We might glance over a story in the news that reports how a fifteen-year-old girl was kidnapped and then found on the "erotic services" section of Craigslist just seven days later after being sold and raped multiple times by paying customers.[1] What do we do with this discrepancy? Usually we just think, "That's sad," but we don't take time to understand why or how it happened—not because we don't care about others, but because we don't see that there is anything we can do to help.

Gary Haugen in his book *Terrify No More* writes, "In the face of overwhelming evil and injustice, we often feel powerless. And that powerlessness paralyzes us and steals our hope."[2] This lack of hope is what we believe causes people to instinctively put their fingers in their ears when what we share is too much for them. It's not because people are insensitive or unloving human beings. It's because they think that what we're sharing will cause them distress and there will be nothing they can do about it except to feel bad.

Just feeling bad about something leaves us hopeless, and we cannot remain in that hopeless state. We must press through it. Haugen says we are paralyzed by hopelessness because we underestimate the value of three things. First, "we underestimate the value of what God has given us to transform lives. Second, we underestimate the value of a single life. And third, we underestimate God's determination to rescue us from a trivial existence if we will just free up our hands and our hearts from unworthy distractions and apply them to matters that make a difference in someone else's life."[3]

Human trafficking is nothing short of pure evil. Anytime someone exploits another person for their own selfish gratification, it dishonors the Creator of all life. But as Haugen so eloquently puts it in the introduction to his book, "I ask you to stick with us through the discomfort caused by some of the subject matter. For in the pain, there is promise; in the hurting, there is hope. And our God is God of justice, who does not turn a deaf ear to the cries of the oppressed. He alone empowers us as we confront the dark world of injustice and experience the joy of rescue, relief, and grace given to those who are suffering."[4]

The God of justice does hear the cries of the oppressed and he wants us to hear them too. As mothers we have discovered that information about sex trafficking hits a particular nerve and is very difficult to learn about, but we believe that in knowing the statistics, understanding the broader issues, and being open to acting from the power we have available to us, we can begin to get thick skin as well as cultivate our tender hearts. With thick skins and tender hearts we'll be prepared to do our part in abolishing slavery and caring for the people God puts before us.

Sex Trafficking

Every minute the most vulnerable women and children around the world are sold for sex, or "raped for profit with impunity," as one author puts it.[5] This is why many people devote their lives to rescuing sex slaves, caring for victims, or working to fix broken government and economic systems. Sex trafficking, according to Victor Malarek, author of *The Johns: Sex For Sale and The Men Who*

Kimberly, Women Who Stand Baltimore women, and a World Relief HIV support group in Cambodia

Buy It, is more than enslavement; "it is modern-day sexual terrorism."[6] Everywhere in the world there are laws stating that sexual exploitation through the use of force or other forms of coercion is illegal.[7] Even in countries as notorious for sex trafficking as Cambodia, there are laws designed to protect children under eighteen years old. The enforcing of these laws is another issue.

A young girl in Thailand whose parents sell her to a trafficker in order to provide food for their family and who is forced to sell her body to Western sex tourists is a victim of sex trafficking. A twenty-two-year-old Russian woman who thinks she is applying for a job at a restaurant in Italy but who instead is gang raped, beaten, drugged and taken to work the streets of Amsterdam is a victim of sex trafficking. A fifteen-year-old girl from Ohio who runs away with her boyfriend, a boy who provides food, shelter and the warmth of his bed until they run out of money and he tells her she must sell her body to earn their next meal—she is a victim of sex trafficking. The eighteen-year-old in India who is put into a room and told she will not receive food until she begins to receive customers for sex is a victim of sex trafficking. The thirteen-year-old from California whose cousin threatens to expose the sex tape he took of her to her parents unless she poses nude for a child porn site is a victim of sex trafficking. The recruitment, the level of violence and the culture may all be different, but by definition each situation is sex trafficking. A better definition yet is slavery.

Poverty and extreme levels of gender inequality play a significant role in why women and children make up more than eighty percent of trafficking victims. Lack of education, low social status and gender discrimination contribute to the viewing of women and children as commodities to be bought and sold.

Despite increased global policy through efforts such as the Trafficking Victims Protection Act and the increased attention the media has given to the subject, sex trafficking still thrives. Sex slavery is big business, generating billions of dollars in profits each year. It has a profit margin higher than almost any other industry in the world, and although experts estimate that sex slaves account for less than five percent of the world's slaves, they generate more than thirty-nine percent of the profits.[8] Due to the lucrative nature of sex trafficking, both small-town criminals and sophisticated organized crime groups have capitalized on this illicit business.

Understanding how and why sex trafficking occurs is helpful in participating in solutions to fight it. Pick up any book or article on poverty, civil unrest, lack of rights for women or refugee camps, and you will read about vulnerable people whose lives are so desperate for survival that when there is a glimmer of a possibility of a job, they will believe the offer to be true. Standing with the most vulnerable, getting a glimpse of the global sex trafficking industry, along with who is fighting to end it—these are what brought Kim to Cambodia.

◆　◆　◆

I wasn't sure how our van was going to fit down the extremely narrow road we had just turned on to. I took a deep breath and listened to our host explain that the people we would be visiting this morning were forced to relocate by their own government. Apparently the government needed the land for development.

It was my second day in Cambodia, and what I saw outside my window confirmed all my fears about coming on this trip in the first place. The extreme poverty I witnessed was in Technicolor. Trash of all colors was tucked in between blades of bright green grass where malnourished, bony cattle tried to graze. Pools of brown muddy water lined the rows of shacks that leaned shoulder to shoulder. I didn't want to get out of the van, but I forced myself to follow the others out. I had met the women I was traveling with only two days ago, so I didn't feel any need to share my thoughts of *Oh my God.* Thankfully no one asked me to.

This is what the statistic of "half of the world lives on less than a dollar a day" looks like, I thought to myself.

Nine tall white women piling out of an air-conditioned van certainly brought attention as local people came out to look and wave hello. The smiles on their faces softened the on-alert tension my body held. I smiled back and took a deep breath as I followed the rest of the group down a small dirt path and into a home where an HIV-AIDS support group was waiting for us.

There was a row of plastic chairs for us to sit in. I found a red plastic stool in the far corner and sat down. I watched as a group of women, three small babies and two of the World Relief team members squeezed onto a raised wooden platform. It was a relief to be in the shade. The shaded interior and proximity to the dirt floor helped us cool off, which aided my ability to listen attentively to what was being translated to us. I was learning a great deal on this trip, including the fact that World Relief has a comprehensive strategy in standing with individuals and working to educate communities about HIV-AIDS and to care for those affected. This support group had grown organically from World Relief's presence in the community.

I was struck by the brutal honesty with which each woman shared. A timid woman explained how she had dropped to fifty-five pounds. A friend finally dragged her to a clinic where she discovered she was HIV-positive. Her husband had had many sexual partners and brought the disease home to her. After finding out she was HIV-positive he left her. But this woman received life-saving medication at the clinic, became healthy and entered a wonderful community of women.

I'm not sure how that platform held all of us, but after an hour of sharing we all gathered on it to pray for one another and to take a picture together. The heaviness that had covered me as I entered the shelter was turned into joy as the sense of community and love those women shared transformed the sharp poverty that stood outside the door.

As I walked back into the bright sun, a small, very dirty girl flashed an all-teeth smile while holding a naked baby on her hip. She asked one of the women in our group with a camera to take her picture. That picture is a reminder of that precious day—the joy of community in the midst of extremely difficult living conditions.

We had another meeting about four hundred yards down the dirt path. This area too was lined with trash. Dogs, cows, cats and other animals roamed around or were asleep in the hot sun. It was here that I learned how in standing with the most vulnerable in Cambodia, World Relief provides an essential weapon in the battle: They train locals on human trafficking prevention.

We filed into the anti–human trafficking training session and sat shoulder to shoulder on the floor with women of all ages from the community. The coordinator explained that today we would learn about the ways people are trafficked. I was impressed by the collaborative efforts of the nonprofit organizations in Cambodia. A Cambodian woman on staff with World Relief taught the class, and the logos of International Justice Mission, World Vision and Chab Dai were on the materials. By working together and sharing resources, these organizations became more effective and able to make a difference.

I was sitting with the most vulnerable. There were sweet little four-year-olds, grandmothers and mothers leaning against a wall. A few men and small children peeked their heads through the door. Witnessing these living conditions, seeing their livestock and hearing stories of disease and relocation, I was beginning to understand how easy it is for human traffickers to deceive people.

There are many ways slaves are acquired by traffickers. Siddharth Kara in his book *Sex Trafficking: Inside the Business of Modern Slavery* highlights five ways sex slaves are acquired globally. Deceit is the most common. This can entail the false offer of a job or even false marriage offers.[9] Children are often trafficked by family members who sell them. Before I saw what desperation looked like firsthand, I could not imagine ever selling my own child. *I would rather all of us die of starvation holding each other than sell one,* I thought to myself.

But as I began to understand a bit of Cambodian history I began to understand how desperation and deceit go hand in hand. Pol Pot and his regime systematically slaughtered every educated person and child, including those who wore eyeglasses or had the appearance of education, for a period of four years. From 1975 to 1979, Pol Pot and his followers killed two million of their own people. At this time the genocide didn't come onto the radar of the rest of world. With the exception of a few organizations, not many groups sent resources into Cambodia to help the remaining people rebuild their country until the 1990s.

Today forty percent of the country lives on less than one dollar a day, making Cambodia one of the poorest countries in Southeast Asia and therefore one of the most vulnerable to human trafficking. Families often believe they have no other options, and that life with someone else may even be better than in the home, so they sell their children.

Extreme poverty is not the only factor that leads families to decide to sell a child. In the United States and in many other countries, addiction is a strong enemy, turning a parent's love into greed. Drug and alcohol addiction can poison a parent's judgment. Desperate to get their next fix they sacrifice the child for money. Most of us cannot imagine this unless we have witnessed a loved one destroying his or her life for the next high—or maybe even experienced it ourselves. We can't imagine just how low a person must become to do this unthinkable act. But it happens.

Abduction is another way people are trafficked. Although abduction is not as frequent as the mainstream media might portray, it does happen both abroad and in the United States.

Women are often trafficked through romance. False promises of love lure vulnerable girls into the arms of slave traders, brothel owners and pimps. Some slave traders woo their victims by buying extravagant gifts. Some even marry their victims. But the end is always the same—sex slavery. Rachel Lloyd, founder of the well-respected nonprofit group GEMS (Girls Educational and Mentoring Services), which works with young victims of commercial sexual exploitation, writes, "If you haven't had proper love and care, then a substitute will feel like the real thing, because you've got nothing to compare it to."[10]

It was encouraging to observe the level of collaboration in Cambodia among organizations that work with trafficking victims. Each organization has a niche and works in the best interest of victims. Some organizations, such as World Relief, work directly with community leaders and the local church in prevention programs. Others, such as International Justice Mission, rescue the victims and prosecute the bad guys. International Justice Mission is one of the only organizations in the world that works with state and local governments to help ensure that public justice systems work effectively to protect the poor and vulnerable. They work with a high level of professionalism and with deep respect for local communities.

I had an opportunity to go on a ride-along with International Justice Mission. Similar to going on a ride-along with a local law enforcement officer in the United States, I simply sat in the backseat of the agent's car and talked with him about what he looks for when building cases and how he knows there is a problem.

I was thankful for the blackout windows. Sitting in the backseat of an SUV I stared undetected down the streets of Phnom Penh. It was nine o'clock at night and I was exhausted from jet lag and the sheer amount of information my mind was trying process. I had been in Cambodia less than a week, yet my heart and mind were weary from everything I had seen and experienced.

Phnom Penh nightlife was just emerging onto the streets. I braced myself, but I wanted to see firsthand what I had only read about in books and articles. Phnom Penh, infamous for its illicit sex tourism industry, was actually outside my car window. Some fear of the unknown rose to the surface, but being with the IJM officer who had taken other civilians out before, I knew I was safe. I was just observing. I was trying to understand.

It soon became evident that no one would need to point out the sex industry to me. It was everywhere—often in neon lights. I felt numb and sick at the same time watching this world pass by. I leaned my forehead against the window and involuntarily gasped. There it was: a beautiful little girl with heavy makeup and long black hair pulled into ponytails sloping down either shoulder. She was sitting sidesaddle on a motor scooter immediately out my window—four feet from me.

She was between two men. A local man drove and a Westerner rode sitting behind the girl. I could see her face. She stared blankly out at the passing cars. I saw her and my heart grieved. I had known what I was going to see tonight and yet I was still stunned. The stereotype of a fifty-year-old white Western sex tourist with a little girl was right in front of me. It made me sick.

We drove on.

My ride-along continued into the most notorious areas in and around Phnom Penh. We drove for an hour around the city, seeing rows of chairs outside small massage parlors where scantily clad Khmer and Vietnamese girls sat waiting for customers. My mind and heart tried to keep up with the images, faces and souls I was passing. I wanted to take note of every young girl whose eyes were still youthful and open. I wanted to remember each teenager and each woman with the numb body language and rote speech.

Earlier in the day I had met with International Justice Mission staff to learn how IJM works in Cambodia and how they collaborate with other organizations on holistic care and restoration for trafficking victims. Things have improved over the last five years in Cambodia. Law enforcement has begun to hold brothel keepers and traffickers accountable. There have been convictions of owners and customers. As a result the trade in young children has become much more risky and less profitable.

The IJM staff informed me that what they see on the streets of Phnom Penh today is very different from the open sale of children they witnessed several years ago. Five years ago it was relatively easy to find a young child being offered. Not so anymore. However, criminals are modifying their methodologies. Many brothels are not operating so publicly, and more "KTVs" and beer gardens are becoming the places to meet women for sale. KTVs, I learned, are karaoke bars. Some large clubs are easy to spot with their blazing neon lights and streets lined with Land Cruisers and Mercedes. These establishments are now the places where it's easiest to find a trafficked woman or girl.

I could see these neon KTVs on the ride-along and I asked the IJM undercover agent just how the process of buying a girl worked.

Turns out it's quite easy. "Customers simply go in and pick out a girl," he explained. "The girls are often behind a glass wall or they're brought out to the table. The girls are wearing numbers and the customers choose which number they want. Then they order a drink."

My mind tried to accept the brazen acceptance of selling girls for rape. I was stunned into silence by the idea that customers would order a girl even before ordering a drink.

The IJM agent continued, "If they want to do more with the girl, they pay a bar fine of about forty dollars and take her to their hotel or another guesthouse."

Like the IJM staff earlier in the day, he explained that over the past five years things have changed a bit. Before, these places operated as straight brothels: a customer would take a girl back to a room on the premises. Since recent action by law enforcement and convictions within the Cambodian judicial system, brothel owners are getting smart and adapting their business.

Taking girls off the premises makes it more difficult for authorities to investigate and build cases; it appears more like two consenting adults leaving together. Even though Cambodian law makes sex with a minor illegal, many people in Cambodia do not have birth certificates to prove their age, and if they do have one, another can be easily forged without detection. Brothel owners and pimps know that it is difficult to demonstrate the real age of many of the girls held captive in these bars. "Many of the girls don't even know how old they are themselves," an IJM staffer told me.

Cambodia is considered a developing country—a country trying to build itself back up after years of genocide and war. It is one of many countries trying to develop a judicial system empowered to create laws and prosecute violators. International Justice Mission trains local law enforcement officers how to conduct effective investigations using the latest techniques and information. IJM team members also work within the Cambodian judicial system, helping local leaders pass effective legislation and uphold the good laws already in place. IJM also has its own highly qualified attorneys who patiently build good cases and walk alongside victims to ensure justice.

IJM and law enforcement workers are often the first to have contact with victims, so they receive sensitivity training that helps them reassure victims they're not in trouble during a rescue but instead are safe. After being rescued, victims are brought to short-term shelters where immediate concerns are addressed and assessments are made regarding their safety. Clients are then transitioned into longer-stay shelters for rehabilitation, health and counseling services, and job training. Clients may stay in these shelters from a few months to three years, depending on their needs for reintegration. The shelters and job training centers are operated by a variety of organizations, such as Hagar International, Daughters of Cambodia and Agape International. They all serve clients in creative ways, working toward whole-person rehabilitation and healing. These shelters are the patient and loving arms of God where hope is found.

In addition to rescue and aftercare, International Justice Mission also provides legal counsel and expertise to trafficking victims. They assist clients in working through the judicial system. This is not a job for the restless and impatient as it requires much acute focus to detail, patience to endure a broken judicial system and wisdom that comes only from bended knee seeking the Lord's divine hand. This is why IJM has the reputation it does. At the same time every day all the International Justice Mission staff—whether in Washington, D.C., Cambodia or Guatemala—stop and pray. They know this kind of evil cannot be stopped by individuals, organizations or governments, but only when God's people join with the Creator of the universe to bring his kingdom on earth as it is in heaven.

It was humbling and inspiring to witness World Relief, IJM and many other groups on the ground acting as a voice for the voiceless and to witness firsthand their tireless fight for justice. Looking at pictures of my time in Cambodia I can get sad and angry knowing there are people profiting by exploiting others' poverty. But I now also know there are good men and women who are committed to standing with the most vulnerable, giving them tools of hope and sustainability, and who fight on their behalf. As one who claims to love the Lord, I believe it is imperative we join them and stand against this evil.

Reflect

1. This chapter deals with one of the most difficult issues within the horror of modern-day slavery. What reaction does this content and these realities create in you?

2. Can you see yourself standing with these victims as a beacon of hope? What would that look like in your life?

Take Action

1. Watch *Trade of Innocents* and work through the companion *Community Abolitionist Guide* with friends (tradeofinnocents.com).

2. Become an IJM FreedomMaker. This is a simple way to create a customized online fundraising campaign—great for both individuals or groups (ijmfreedommaker.org).

3. Visit freetheslaves.net and sign up to receive email updates.

Not in My Backyard

Kimberly McOwen Yim

> *Some of us, like old Wilberforce on the subject of slavery,*
> *are actually called to bore the pants off people by going on and on about*
> *it until eventually the point is taken and the world is changed.*

N. T. WRIGHT, *SURPRISED BY HOPE*

The San Clemente Abolitionist Mamas were meeting with our friend Doug and his business partner, Jason, to discuss a logo design and website idea we had recently been thinking about. We had been throwing ideas around since our first event and we were finally taking time to discuss them with the best marketing guys we knew.

In our meeting we shared that we were concerned about the many new "massage" businesses that had recently opened in our area, indicating to us that more was going on in our beach town than we'd realized. Doug doubted that sex trafficking was occurring in our hometown of San Clemente, so we impulsively posed him a challenge.

"I bet you can find it online. Go to OCWeekly.com and type in 'adult services' and see what you find searching our zip code," I suggested.

He did. Thirty seconds later Doug spun his laptop around to show us the screen.

"No way," he said.

The screen read, "Relaxation massage" followed by an address. Around the text were four pictures of women's breasts.

Doug suggested that although illegal, what the "massage" ad was pointing to was simply prostitution and not sex trafficking.

"There may be a small percentage of women who truly choose to work in the commercial sex industry," replied Tracy, one of the San Clemente abolitionists, "but considering that the average age when a commercial sex worker turns her first trick is between the ages of eleven and thirteen, then most commercial sex workers are victims. Maybe not all, but most."

Now our adrenalin was pumping. This was exactly why we continued to talk with our family and friends and host community events. Our time and resources were very limited, but this kind of conversation motivated us to press on and continue doing what we could.

We Googled the address of the massage ad and were sickened when we realized where it was. It was right in the center of our town, next to my church and its preschool. It was behind one of the most popular Italian restaurants in the city. Many high school students walked by it on their way to school each day. It was in my backyard.

Commercial sexual exploitation gets a lot of press these days, due to the known profits of the industry and its saturation in our culture. We have been tolerant due to the deep respect we have for the freedom of speech and for diversity and personal values. "What is right for me may not be right for you" has merit and should be protected under law, yet violence, exploitation and enslavement of others should not be.

Discovering the truth about whether or not someone is enslaved often begins with asking questions. Is she being coerced into doing this? Is she being deceived into providing this service? Is she being held against her will? Is she free to walk away?

We have been conditioned to mind our own business, enabling modern slavery to flourish right in front of our eyes. Three years ago I would never have thought to ask the young girl walking downtown at midnight in a short minidress and stilettos if she wanted to be there. I would have never wondered if she was being beaten at night for not fulfilling her nightly quota. The questions never crossed my mind.

I've always hated that our society has so many strip clubs, which exist to fulfill the fantasy of our sex-crazed culture. But the thought of whether the women were being abused or working to pay off a never-ending debt had never occurred to me. I assumed that everyone has different values and we all make our own choices based on what we think is best for ourselves. It never crossed by mind to ask, "Can they walk away? Are they slaves?"

A month after the Abolitionist Mamas meeting with our Web designer friends, I was driving home from an appointment and stopped at a red light across from the massage parlor we'd discovered online. *I wonder if our suspicions are true,* I thought to myself.

My kids weren't in the car, so I impulsively decided to go check it out. I pulled into the little parking lot and casually got out of my car. My heart was racing. I wasn't sure if this was a good idea.

I opened the door. My heart sank. It did not open into a reception area. Behind the first door was another metal steel door. I squinted, trying to see through the small holes of the grated door. I slowly turned the knob. It was locked, despite the neon "open" sign out front. I had just watched a report on the news about how these types of establishments operate. The program revealed that locked doors speak to illegal activities taking place inside. Pedestrian traffic and the general public are not welcome.

I called, "Hello! Hello! Anyone there?"

With my face pressed against the locked metal door, I waited. Eventually I saw a short Asian women walking quickly toward me. She didn't seem very threatening, but she did appear annoyed.

"Yes? What do you want?" She opened the door but stood in the middle of the doorway.

"Do you have a menu of massage options I can look at?" I stammered, trying to sound casual and calm. My heart was pumping.

"No," she said. She just stood there.

There was a bit of awkward silence, then I stammered some more about coming back when I had more time—I was looking for a new place to get a massage as my last therapist had moved away. I'm a terrible liar.

"Thanks!" I said cheerfully. "I'll be back." Walking to my car I took two pictures of the cars parked in the lot.

When I got a few miles away from the massage parlor, I pulled over and called the National Human Trafficking Hotline Number: 888-373-7888. The hotline is a program of the Polaris Project, a leading anti-trafficking organization. Operating twenty-four hours a day, seven days a week, the hotline is a great resource for reporting a tip, connecting with anti-trafficking services in your area and requesting training, general information and other anti-trafficking resources.

When I called, I relayed everything I knew about the place: from the OCWeekly.com ad that had tipped us off not everything was okay with this business, to my current experience with the locked door and the woman's suspicious behavior. The woman who received my call took my tip seriously, asked follow-up questions and recommended that I notify my local law enforcement agency as well.

Four months later the place was still open and I was frustrated. In time I called the local Orange County Human Trafficking Task Force and talked with an officer who works with the group. He put me in touch with the local undercover police officer who handles these issues in our area.

The local law enforcement officer confirmed my concern and said this massage parlor was a known venue for prostitution, but due to a lack of resources it had been hard to build a case against it. He assured me that now that he knew people in the community were concerned, he would make it a priority. Over a year later, the place was still operating.

Let me make it very clear that I'm not recommending that ordinary people conduct investigations and put themselves in harm's way trying to get answers to their questions. This is the role of law enforcement. However, the average person can slow down and observe. If we pay a bit more attention to our surroundings, we might be surprised by the number of "doesn't seem quite right" activities taking place in our communities.

If something seems out of place or "not quite right," call the national anti-trafficking hotline and your local police department. Don't brush it under the rug. Take the time to report any suspicious activity. If something is not reported, law enforcement doesn't know to be concerned about it. The national hotline provides resources to those who have questions, makes referrals to those at risk, and collects information and statistics for the U.S. State Department. The hotline also works in partnership with local human trafficking task forces. It's important to memorize or have quick access to the hotline number: 888-373-7888.

Human trafficking is happening in our backyards. Do we give in to the status quo of minding our own business? My friends and I remain committed to a no-slavery policy in our city; and although we can't devote ourselves full time to this struggle, we can chip away at it by asking questions, calling the national hotline and talking to our neighbors.

Reflect

1. Do you think slavery is in your backyard? Why or why not?

2. How can you discover, fight and inform your community about slavery in your city or community?

Take Action

1. Learn the National Hotline Number: 888-373-7888.

2. Visit www.polarisproject.org and find out if there's an anti-trafficking task force in your area.

Who's Buying?

Kimberly McOwen Yim

The average time it takes for a runaway child to be
approached by a trafficker is 48 hours.

POLARIS PROJECT

"Come on! You have to go with me!" Tracy said enthusiastically over the phone.

I didn't have a good excuse not to go. And I knew her husband would probably feel better knowing that Tracy had a friend along while she was walking the streets of Anaheim, California, for street training. Saddleback Church in nearby Laguna Hills was just beginning to form an anti-trafficking team, and they had brought in an expert to offer training on how to approach a woman or girl being sexually exploited and offer her assistance out of the life.

We didn't have any expectations about where we were going or what we would learn. We were simply going to absorb as much as we could in order to better understand what was going on in the world of human trafficking and perhaps to learn something we could pass on to the rest of the Abolitionist Mamas and those who attended our events.

What we learned that night opened the door to how sex trafficking is occurring right in our own backyards and how the most vulnerable victims are teens and pre-teens. Tracy and I both have pre-teen daughters and this night hit us hard.

I wasn't surprised to learn about the psychological factors and history of abuse that many sexually exploited children have endured, but I did not know the extent to which there was a real subculture of sexually exploited youth. I had heard the expression "Who's your daddy?" and I had heard through mainstream media about there being a "pimp culture," but I never connected the dots before to sex slavery of women and children until that night.

Both of our trainers that evening shared in general terms that much of what they knew and what fueled their educational efforts was a result of their own life experience. I didn't know quite what that meant until we actually hit the streets of Anaheim and began to put our training into action in groups of three and four.

"You always go with a male," our trainer explained. "He walks a few paces behind and watches you and your surroundings." Tracy remained with the male of our group, a retired police officer. I walked ahead with Lauri, an unassuming twenty-something with a sweet face and long brown hair. I was curious to learn how she had become committed to helping children get out of "the life," as we learned it is called.

We walked past rows of run-down motels. While learning about the culture of commercially sexually exploited boys and girls, we could see the sign: "The Happiest Place on Earth." Just steps from Disneyland was hell.

We began to see young kids, sometimes with their mom or older siblings just hanging out. There were young children in the parking lots of these motels at eleven o'clock at night. What was going on?

Lauri explained that young girls called the men who exploited them their "daddies," demonstrating the desperate need for family that was present within this subculture. Other family-type terms were "wife-in-law," or "wifey," referring to other girls who were exploited by the same pimp. It was apparent that women and children were more susceptible to violence than men. The language used reflected this reality. Women and girls were referred to as "hos" and "bitches," whereas the men who abused, raped, beat and exploited them were called "pimps," "daddies" and "johns."

Some may say that what we really learned about that night was teen prostitution, not sex trafficking. Four years ago I might have agreed. But new legislation passed by Congress has helped change the language of child sex trafficking in the United States. What used to be referred to as juvenile prostitution is now referred to as "commercial sexual exploitation of children" (CSEC). The act of manipulating a child into prostitution is now referred to as "child sex trafficking," and those who were once called pimps are now referred to as "traffickers." This shift in language has helped create a paradigm shift, reducing the tendency to blame the victim and to properly characterize the trafficker and customer as the ones committing a serious crime.

As a society we have determined time and time again, as supported by extensive research, that all children need to be protected. Whether or not a teen is a sassy-mouthed, rebellious, bratty teenager is not the point. He or she is a minor—a child—and needs and deserves protection.

"There's a reason that we have age limits and standards governing the 'choices' that children and youth can make, from drinking to marrying to driving to leaving school, and it's because as a society we recognize that there's a difference between child/adolescent development and adult development," writes Rachel Lloyd, founder of GEMS and author of *Girls Like Us*.[1] As a society we know that children and adolescents don't have the psychological development to make the best decisions for themselves. They need adults to protect them.

The average age of a person who is first recruited into commercial sex work is between eleven and thirteen years old. That means that almost every man, woman and child that we learn is in some type of commercial sex work is a victim of sexual abuse and sex trafficking. Instead of being protected by an adult in their life, they were exploited by one.

It is important to note that adults who sexually exploit women and children are not only stereotypical pimps; they can be also brothel owners, parents, strip club owners, pornographers, members of organized crime, boyfriends or online "adult service" providers. They can be any age, gender or ethnicity.

After an hour of walking, we rounded the corner of our last street. Lauri expressed disappointment that we hadn't seen many of the girls she knew were out here.

"It's okay," I said. "I'm surprised we saw what we did. I sure did get a glimpse into the conditions that those who are most vulnerable to trafficking are living in."

"Yeah, I guess," Lauri said, although she was clearly frustrated. "I know this area well," she said. After a long pause, she continued, "Just down six blocks from here was once my track."

"The track," we had learned, was the street or area in which a commercially exploited woman or girl worked. I didn't know how to respond. Looking at her sweet face, porcelain skin and kind brown eyes, I could not picture her former life on the streets.

She continued, "This is why I know so much."

Looking back on that night I see just how much hope Lauri represents in a situation that at times seems bleak.

After thanking our training leaders, we were just stepping into Tracy's car ready to head back home when we heard the honk of a horn on the main street. We turned and witnessed a girl about fifty feet from us, dressed in a tight green minidress and spiked black heels and wearing heavy makeup, open the door to a forest-green SUV and step inside. We both tried to see the driver, but it was too dark.

It had happened in less than twenty seconds. We soberly got into Tracy's car and drove away in silence.

Who was the guy driving the green SUV? I wondered. The girl was easy to spot in her tight, bright green dress and heels on a curb at midnight. But the person driving was behind tinted windows.

The men who create the demand for sex trafficking lurk in the shadows, hiding behind tinted windows or a computer screen and a fake name. They never offer up their real identities. With outright cowardice they create the foundation of this thirty-two-billion-dollar global business—a business that makes its wealth on the exploitation of the most vulnerable.

We have talked about the supply side, the commoditization of women and children who are in extreme poverty or other desperate circumstances. On the demand side we find men. Without men willing to pay for sex we would have no need for a supply. It is demand that fuels modern-day sex slavery.

In understanding the demand side of the sex slave trade, Donna M. Hughes in her 2004 study "Best Practices to Address the Demand Side of Sex Trafficking" mentions three factors: the men who pay for sex; the profiteers, such as traffickers, pimps and brothel owners; and a culture that "indirectly creates a demand for victims by normalizing prostitution."[2] In this book we won't attempt to comment much on those who profit from the sale of women and children for sex. "The love of money is a root of all kinds of evil," Paul writes in 1 Timothy 6:10. Sex trafficking is the manifestation of how dark a soul can become when one is willing to sell another human life for selfish financial gain. But we will comment on the men who consume and how our culture's romanticizing of sexual exploitation contributes to the growing violence against women and children.

One of the most difficult books to read about human trafficking is Victor Malarek's *The Johns: Sex For Sale and the Men Who Buy It.* What's difficult is not the vocabulary or the style but how complete an understanding one gains of the men who are willing to buy sex. Malarek concludes, "What we are witnessing today is nothing less than international sexual terrorism against women and children at the hands of men, and little is being done to stop the carnage."[3]

"Sexual terrorism" may seem a strong term. But Dr. Melissa Farley in a study published in the *Journal of Trauma Practice* in 2003 found that after interviewing 854 prostituted women from nine different countries, sixty-eight percent of them met the criteria for post-traumatic stress disorder. This finding is in the same range as combat veterans and victims of state-organized torture.[4]

Men who are willing to pay for sex are often called "johns." It is a name of anonymity, keeping them in the shadow of the global sex trade. Online sex boards are where johns find community. They refer to themselves as "hobbyists." Most men buying sex are ordinary guys who come from a variety of backgrounds and occupations. Some are teenagers and young twenty-year-olds who visit a brothel in order to lose their virginity. Others might be retired college professors, megachurch pastors or successful businessmen. Every age and nationality is present among men who are willing to pay for sex.

Malarek mentions that some men may regret buying sex and some may not, but throughout the world the attitudes are similar: These men's wants, needs and desires reign supreme. "Entitlement, power, and control are the common factors when men search for paid sex."[5]

Entitlement, power and control play out differently with each john. Some cultures have accepted the commonly held view that "boys will be boys" and are entitled to sex. In some societies it is an accepted way to bond with friends. Whereas some men come together over a pitcher of beer while watching a football game, others bond at a brothel or with a few sexually exploited girls at a strip club. Some married johns who pay for sex may claim to love their wives and have a sex life with her, but they want something different outside the marriage and believe they deserve it. Some men are single and for whatever reason cannot cultivate a healthy relationship. There are others who desire the illusion of a girlfriend and who are willing to pay for it.

Many men go to great lengths and distances to get these desires met. Some play ignorant to the plight of the women they are with, while others are simply misogynists who take pleasure in dominance and violence. Some even claim they're doing these women and children a favor since the money will go toward food and shelter. Regardless of why they're willing to pay for sex, all johns believe they're entitled to do whatever they want to the woman or child they're with. This is why commercial sex workers are at high risk for assault, rape, battery and murder.

So what is being done to stop the demand? Some countries have criminalized the purchase of sex acts, such as Sweden in 1998. (In fact, Sweden criminalized the purchase of sex at about the same time many other European countries legalized prostitution.) In Sweden commercial sex work is defined as male violence against women, so the government decriminalized the selling of sex and made the buying of sex a crime. Women were no longer at risk of arrest and prosecution for prostitution, but the men who tried to buy sex began to be held criminally responsible. Within four years of this law's passing, the number of women working in the sex trade in Sweden had been cut in half. Ten years later, only five hundred or so women are trafficked per year, whereas neighboring countries—much smaller countries—see anywhere from five thousand to twelve thousand trafficking victims yearly.[6]

Siddharth Kara, after examining all the different policies held by countries in regard to sex trafficking, would choose "the stance of the U.S. and Swedish governments: the criminalization of prostitution, including the purchase of sex acts and the owning, operating, or financing of sex establishments." In addition, Kara says, there is a continued need for governments, law enforcement and communities to remain vigilant for signs of prostitution, regardless of the challenges.[7]

Within the United States there are more people joining Malarek and Farley in researching and raising awareness of the men who buy sex, the marketplace for sex trafficking and the social implications of the saturated commercial sex industry. Still other people are concentrating on the education of young boys by using new age-appropriate curriculum to teach boys how to respect and honor their bodies and to respect and honor girls and their bodies.

Some people are working toward shutting down easy online accessibility to sex slavery through such venues as Backpage.com. In 2010 we saw Craigslist finally shut down its "adult services" and "erotic" sections. Still, larger publications such as the *Village Voice*, which owns Backpage, and smaller newspapers and websites such as my local OCWeekly.com continue to profit at a rate of $33 million per year from sexual services ads, which provide easy access to exploited women and children.

Faith communities are getting involved in the fight against demand by educating pastors and congregations and training them how to combat the problem in their own communities. Organizations such as International Justice Mission, Free the Slaves and the Not for Sale campaign provide focused tools and resources to help church leaders bring congregations together to address the problem.

Demand is also being addressed through "john school." Like

traffic school, john school is a one-day option for first-time offenders who are arrested for soliciting paid sex. There are about fifty schools across the country. The offender pays a fine of anywhere from $100 to $1,000, then sits through an eight-hour session listening to speakers such as nurses who teach about the realities of HIV-AIDS and other STDs, social workers who work with women and children who've been in the commercial sex business, and women who've been commercially sexually exploited.

Some law enforcement agencies and other organizations are using technology to decrease the demand. These groups use the same methods as perpetrators to locate sexually exploited women and children, creating decoy ads or building false relationships with johns as a way to bring them into the light and make arrests. Another community might suspend a john's driver license or confiscate his car. And in other areas you might hear or see a public service announcements that begins, "Dear Johns," then goes on to describe the plight of exploited women and girls or explain the risk of contracting an STD.

Legislators are making great strides in decreasing the demand. New state bills are being introduced and passed to increase penalties for the solicitation of sex for sale as well as for all forms of commercial sexual exploitation of children. More and more people are becoming aware of the issue and are using public policies to make their opinion and concern known. In April 2003 the U.S. Congress passed the PROTECT (Prosecutorial Remedies and Other Tools to End the Exploitation of Children Today) Act. This act enables U.S. authorities to arrest Americans who sexually abuse children abroad and prosecute them under U.S. laws. There have been a number of successful convictions under this act.[8]

Law enforcement plays a crucial role in ending the demand. Agencies across the country are being trained to enforce laws effectively and collaborate with social services. Historically, women and children have been seen as the criminals and they were the ones prosecuted. This is changing as more law enforcement agencies are adapting their tactics to address the demand side of the problem.

To fully address the issue of demand, we must address pornography. The glorification of pimps and the pornographication of our lives is more than a moral dilemma we must navigate. It is intrinsically linked to the slavery of millions. Every book or article that specifically addresses sex trafficking claims that pornography and other forms of commercial sexual exploitation such as strip clubs are connected to sexual slavery. We are not saying that every woman stripping or every man in a porn film is being held against his or her will, but there is no doubt that wherever sex is being commercially sold, there are individuals who do not want to be there.

Malarek does not mince words when he writes, "While the porn industry tries to sell its product as a form of sexual liberation, free speech, and artistic expression, pornography is in essence prostitution, because it involves the purchase of another person's body for sexual gratification. Therefore, the men who buy and watch porn are themselves johns."[9] Pornography today is not a world where men and women are equal or where bodies are admired for their beauty. It is a world where women are dominated, urinated on, spit upon, beaten and raped. But we are told pornography is a matter of personal choice and something people engage with in private. We keep silent because the world has told us we are prudish if we voice our concern about the effects pornography has on our children or our society.

Far too often people simply don't want to know. "Boys will be boys," we hear friends say as they brush the pain of their husband's porn habit under the rug. But pornography is a serious issue and needs to be addressed by individuals, couples and broader communities. What kind of people are we—what kind of society are we—if we turn our heads to violence and degradation enacted for the sexual pleasure of others?

As a mother, I am troubled by studies showing that the first online exposure to porn happens at eleven years of age and that thirty-five percent of boys aged thirteen and fourteen say they've viewed pornographic Internet content "too many times to count."[10] Once a tolerance for a certain type of pornography is built up, boredom kicks in and the user experiences an inability to get the same sexual satisfaction. This is why there is a fast-growing market for violent and humiliating pornography that features women suffering and being punished. "Some scenes are so vile they don't even resemble what we know as sex," writes Malarek—what's on the Internet today is not even close to the *Playboy* style of pornography one might think of.[11] Deviant types of pornography that feed on dark fetishes such as bondage, pregnant women, animals, violence and young children is big Internet business.

Child pornography is one of the fastest-growing crimes in the United States right now. Nationally, there has been a 2,500 percent increase in arrests in the past ten years, according to the FBI. The National Center for Missing and Exploited Children (NCMEC), which helps to identify and locate children in pornography photos and videos, has reviewed and analyzed almost 30 million photos and videos of child pornography since 2003.[12] The NCMEC reviews and assesses approximately 250,000 child pornography images and videos per week. "The problem of child pornography has become epidemic," says president and CEO Ernie Allen. "And the victims are getting younger and the abuse more brutal."[13] (If you ever come into contact with any young-looking or child pornography, please call 800-843-5678 or visit cybertipline.com.)

Pornography is the entry point for being willing to pay for sex. There is a link between what is observed in porn and what johns seek to buy in a real human being. After interviewing women in prostitution in nine countries, Melissa Farley found that forty-seven percent were upset by the johns' attempts to make them do what they had seen in pornography.[14]

We need to talk about this. First, we need to talk to our spouses about the subject. Many marriages have already suffered due to pornography addiction in the home. We also need to have the courage to bring it up with our sons and daughters. We must be diligent in protecting our kids, even if that requires us to hyper-monitor their social media and texting activities. We must teach our children to be educated consumers and wise users of technology, and we must be candid and specific about the world's evils. We must clearly articulate the goodness of sex and God's original design, but we must be blunt in explaining that people will distort this design and will target them.

It is within your power to teach your children to be on alert and to know what to do when they come across pornographic material or when they're approached by an online "friend" they do not know. Talk openly about it and be willing to act accordingly. Don't be afraid. Engage. Refuse to tolerate any part of society where there is buying or selling of human flesh. People are not for sale.

Reflect

1. What can we teach our sons and daughters that would help bring an end to sex trafficking?

2. What can we teach our children that will make them less vulnerable?

3. What are some contributing factors in our culture that make abolishing commercial sexual exploitation difficult?

Take Action

1. Go to ijm.org and download the Community Justice Assessment tool. Use it to examine justice issues in your own community and discuss how your church or group can be part of the solution.

2. Attend a meeting with a local anti-trafficking task force.

3. Go to missingkids.com to become informed on what that organization is doing to protect children. Put the number for their twenty-four-hour hotline (800-843-5678) into your phone in case you or your children come across an image or video of a young adult or child being sexually exploited. (Or you can report it at cypbertipline.com.)

Be the Nosy Neighbor

Kimberly McOwen Yim

> *The best defense against modern-day slavery*
> *is a vigilant public. Be a nosy neighbor.*
>
> KEVIN BALES, *THE SLAVE NEXT DOOR*

Told they will have good-paying jobs when they arrive in the United States, thousands of immigrants, both legal and illegal, get tricked into forced labor annually. Traffickers often deceive these people by offering half-truths, saying the individual will work at a restaurant or in a hotel. Once these people begin working, they are held captive either through never-ending debt or simple physical immobility. Without knowing the language or having someone to trust and under constant threat of physical violence, these workers silently go about working in the background of public businesses.

In Homes

Although eighty percent of human trafficking cases in the United States between 2008 and 2010 were sex trafficking cases, not all modern forms of slavery are related to sex trafficking.[1] A more subtle form of slavery found in our backyards is the enslavement of domestic help. "One of the most insidious forms of trafficking—the enslavement of domestics and nannies—occurs under our very noses. Here you must be vigilant," write coauthors Bales and Soodalter.[2] Often working up to sixteen hours a day, victims of domestic servitude make up the second-highest form of slavery in the United States.[3] Most are foreigners and work under threats of violence. Afraid to run away, they often work in isolation due to a language barrier or lack of interaction with others. Domestic slaves live quietly in fear—fear of deportation, fear of beatings, fear of the well-being of other family members or fear of humiliation. This fear keeps domestic slaves hidden and submissive.

Such was the case in one of the first accounts I heard of in my neck of the woods in Southern California. This case occurred more than ten years ago, before the Trafficking Victims Protection Act was voted into law, and therefore our courts had to wrestle through the rescue and rehabilitation of a child domestic slave.

Shyima was one of twelve children, originally from Egypt, when she was sold to another Egyptian family at eight years old. This family eventually moved to the United States and settled in a gated community in Irvine, California. Shyima slept on a mattress on the floor of the garage and was not allowed to go to school. She spent each day cooking and cleaning and caring for the family's three children from morning until night. Her captors told her they would kill her family if she tried to flee or if she told anyone about her situation. They also told her law enforcement would beat her and take her to jail. So rather than trusting the police for help, she feared them. For two years Shyima lived as a domestic slave in the United States, rarely stepping outside the door of the house where she worked. Eventually an anonymous tip—possibly from a neighbor—was called in to child protective services, and law enforcement got involved.[4]

Years later when Shyima was an adult she was interviewed for a training video to teach others what domestic slavery might look like. She said not knowing the language, fear of law enforcement, and physical and psychological threats were what kept her from running away. "Who would I run to? What would I say? There was nobody for me to trust," she explained.

Thankfully, Shyima's story is a hopeful one. She was adopted by a loving family, enrolled in school and eventually graduated from high school. Now she is attending college with the dream of becoming a law enforcement officer. She has a special interest in rescuing other trafficking victims.

Many stories have been uncovered recently about domestic slaves eventually finding freedom. Some risk it all and run, but many are rescued because of the action of a nosy neighbor. These nosy neighbors are Good Samaritans who reach out to help when something just doesn't seem right. "Slavery often comes to light because a member of the public sees something odd and speaks up," write Bales and Soodalter.[5]

In Fields

In the United States most workers are protected by the National Labor Relations Act of 1935. This law gives workers the right to organize and protects against unsafe work environments, fixed wages and health issues. It applies to all kinds of work—but not farm labor. Because of reasons steeped in Deep South politics, farm laborers and household servants were excluded from full rights.[6]

As you can imagine, this has had tremendous impact on agricultural work standards in the United States, where competitive prices and cheap labor can quickly lead to forced slave labor. Abysmal working conditions in the tomato fields of southern Florida led to the formation of the Coalition of Immokalee Workers (CIW). Southwest Florida is the state's most important center for agricultural production, and Immokalee is the state's largest farmworker community. Many Immokalee workers come from Mexico, Latin America and Haiti. Formed in the 1990s to organize for fair wages and to combat other labor violations, the CIW began to discover well-networked slavery operations. The organization continued to fight for fairer wages and labor practices, but it also began to uncover, investigate and assist in the federal prosecution of slavery rings preying on farm workers. Working with the Department of Justice and the FBI, the CIW has helped to prosecute seven major cases of Florida's tomato farms, freeing over twelve hundred people from captivity and forced labor.[7] Through its efforts the CIW has brought the terrible state of human rights in much of U.S. agriculture today to public light.

Although slavery is not the norm in agriculture today, there must be more of a concerted effort in addressing the demand side of the U.S. food market. Major food-buying corporations are profiting from extremely low—often artificially low—cost of produce.

In the summer of 2012, International Justice Mission partnered with the Coalition of Immokalee Workers for a campaign they called Recipe for Change. Recognizing that for decades slavery and other human rights abuses have existed in U.S. tomato fields, IJM and CIW assert that our local supermarkets can help end slavery in the tomato supply chain. Supermarkets can join with other companies such as McDonalds and Subway by participating in the Fair Food Program.

Developed by the tomato pickers themselves, the Fair Food Program establishes a zero-tolerance policy for slavery, child labor and sexual abuses on Florida's tomato fields. Corporations that join the Fair Food Program agree to pay a small price increase (1.5 cents more per pound) for fairly harvested tomatoes and promise to shift purchases to the Florida tomato growers who abide by these higher standards—and away from those who won't.

Although many fast food companies have already joined the Fair Food Program, some of the largest U.S. supermarket chains have not. IJM's Recipe for Change campaign is asking anti-slavery advocates to petition supermarkets to do their part and join the Fair Food Programs. As of June 2012 Trader Joe's and Whole Foods were the only two major supermarket chains that had joined.

This campaign is an excellent example of how with a little bit of knowledge the consumer has immense power. By going to IJM's website, an individual can send a message to the large U.S. supermarkets asking for their participation in the Fair Food Program. You can sign up to receive email updates on the progress of the campaign and download a petition that asks others in the community to join in. In addition, a family action kit is available on the IJM site that includes information, games and stories for the whole family to learn and participate in the work of justice for agricultural workers.[8]

In Restaurants

David Batstone, an ethics professor in San Francisco, first encountered the reality that slavery existed in his backyard after a eating at one of his favorite restaurants outside of Berkeley. Not long after dining at the restaurant, he read in a local paper that a woman who worked there had died due to a gas leak and lack of ventilation in the apartment attached to the restaurant. Threatening to reveal their illegal status, the owner of the restaurant had forced a number of people to work for him without pay. This revelation prompted Batstone to look further into the issue of modern-day slavery and write a book on his findings, and in 2007 he launched Not For Sale, a campaign whose purpose is to put a final end to slavery.

My friend Tracy recently asked the woman who cleans her house, Elise, how she immigrated to the United States. Tracy learned that Elise originally came over on a work visa to work in a restaurant in Orange County. When she began work, the manager took her documents and told her she'd get them back after she'd worked there for six years. Tracy voiced her concern and asked many more questions, but Elise told her it had worked out okay for her and her husband; they worked at the restaurant for six years and were both able to become legal citizens. "But I do fear for the others still there," Elise said. "The manager has become more strict and it is not a good place to work."

Tracy asked Elise if she would consider telling the police about what the manager was doing. She explained that it was illegal and under the Trafficking Victims Protection Act her friend would be able to get some help, even if she came here illegally. Elise told Tracy she didn't trust the police. "Where I come from the police often do nothing or they make it worse," she said.

Knowing that she would not be able to convince Elise to report what she knew, Tracy contacted the Orange County Human Trafficking Task Force. She was put in touch with a law enforcement agent who took down all the details. A few months later Tracy followed up to see how the case was coming. "Let's just say it was a very good tip," the officer said. He couldn't tell her much more, but Tracy now understood that she could do something—that sometimes a small act such as a phone call could make a difference.

Modern-day slavery is happening right under our noses and yet we often don't see it. Do we know what to look for? What questions do we ask? What do "doesn't seem right" and "something odd" look like?

It's true that we are busy. We run to the carpool line, pick up dry cleaning, go to the grocery store, and we often don't notice the many people we encounter as we go through our days. Despite this, we all have time to call the National Human Trafficking Hotline number if we notice something suspicious: 888-373-7888. Take a minute and enter this number into your cell phone contacts list.

Below is a list of everyday places where slavery has been documented in the United States, as well as signs that someone may be a human trafficking victim. As you read through the list, keep in mind the places and people around your town who work in these types of environments. You may want to mark or copy these pages for future reference. Also, please put the National Human Trafficking Hotline number in your phone and address book: 888-373-7888. Did we mention this already? Yep, and it is that important.

Where to Look for Slavery

Here are some common places and situations where slavery has been known to flourish:

- Housecleaning services
- Landscape and gardening businesses
- Households in which domestic home workers are present
- Large-scale agricultural operations
- Construction sites
- Casinos
- Garment factories
- Hotels (especially in housekeeping departments)
- Nail salons
- Migrant or transitional communities
- Zones known for prostitution
- Strip clubs
- Massage parlors
- Domestic violence situations

Following are some signs that someone might be a human trafficking victim. Any one of these signs should be enough to raise concern and a reason to call the National Human Trafficking Hotline or local law enforcement. A person might be a human trafficking victim if he or she

- is not free to come and go as he or she wishes
- is not free to change employers
- is afraid to discuss him or herself in the presence of others
- does not control his or her earnings
- is unpaid, paid very little or paid only through tips
- has few or no personal possessions
- is not in control of his or her own money or has no financial records or bank account
- is not in control of his or her own identification documents (e.g., ID, passport, visa)
- is not allowed or able to speak for himself or herself (i.e., a third party insists on being present or interpreting)
- has an attorney that he or she doesn't seem to know or to have agreed to receive representation services from
- works excessively long or unusual hours
- is not allowed breaks or suffers under unusual restrictions at work
- owes a large or increasing debt and is unable to pay it off
- was recruited through false promises concerning the nature and conditions of his or her work
- is living or working in a location with high security measures (e.g., opaque or boarded-up windows, bars on windows, barbed wire, security cameras)

- exhibits unusually fearful, anxious, depressed, submissive, tense, nervous or paranoid behavior

- reacts with unusually fearful or anxious behavior at any reference to law enforcement

- avoids eye contact

- exhibits a flat affect (e.g., doesn't display emotion, seems blank or empty, unresponsive)

- exhibits unexplained injuries or signs of prolonged or untreated illness or disease

- appears malnourished

- is under eighteen years of age and is providing commercial sex acts

- is in the commercial sex industry and has a pimp or manager

- shows signs of physical or sexual abuse, physical restraint, confinement or torture

- has been "branded" by a trafficker (e.g., a tattoo of the trafficker's name)

- claims to be "just visiting" and is unable to clarify where he or she is

- exhibits a lack of knowledge of whereabouts or does not know what city he or she is in

- exhibits a loss of a sense of time

- has numerous inconsistencies in his or her story

In addition, a young person might be caught up in sex trafficking if he or she

- has unexplained absences from school for a period of time

- is unable to attend school on a regular basis

- repeatedly runs away from home
- makes references to frequent travel to other cities
- exhibits bruises or other physical trauma, withdrawn behavior, depression or fear
- lacks control over her or his schedule or identification documents
- is hungry or malnourished and inappropriately dressed based on weather conditions or surroundings
- shows signs of drug addiction[9]

When we first learned of the millions of people enslaved in our world today, we wished we were young again, when we thought we could take on the world. We were fired up and wanted to correct injustice. But we grieved because we thought there was not a thing we could do.

We wanted supernatural abilities to fight the bad guys. We may have even wanted to punch a bad guy in the face. We wanted to personally rescue a child out of slavery and hold her in our arms and tell her everything would be okay. We wanted to save people from this life of terror. After all, we lived blessed lives. We needed to do something. But "joining the fight against human trafficking means accepting that we each have a job to do and that our job might not include being the action hero," Bales reminds us.[10]

Once we got over the desire to find a grandiose response to the injustices of slavery and to punch bad guys in the face, we moved forward in the small, meaningful actions that are needed every day. We came to realize we could help right where we were, right in this season of life, right in our neighborhoods—we are the cement in this modern abolitionist movement. We continue to be busy moms; however, today we live our lives intentionally aware of our surroundings and our neighbors. Slavery still exists in my backyard, but I know now I have resources and power to fight it.

Reflect

1. What surprised you when reading this chapter?

2. Are there places in your own community that you now wonder might be places where people are forced to work?

Take Action

1. Put the National Human Trafficking Hotline number in your phone: 888-373-7888. If a person or situation came to mind while you were reading the list of signs of human trafficking, call now and report it.

2. Tell one friend about the anti-trafficking hotline and ask her to put it in her phone.

Congo, Your Phone and Child Slaves

Kimberly McOwen Yim

> *How can you eat, how can you drink,*
> *How wear your finery, and ne'er think*
> *Of those poor souls, in bondage held,*
> *Whose painful labor is compelled?*

ANONYMOUS

We are a technology-loving people. We love our computers, our smart phones, our iPads and MP3 players. We may not be proud of it, but part of our identity is formed by the technology we carry and use. Scripture says that where you put your treasure, there will be your heart (Matthew 6:21). Therefore we must conclude that we love our technological devices. We may love God, our families, our friends and our freedoms more, but as measured by the dollar amount we spend in a year on technology, we must admit we love our technology too. Our devices are second nature to us, like additional limbs. We rely on them like we rely on clean water coming out of our kitchen faucets. We carry our iPhones with us at all time and use them all day long. Making calls, coordinating schedules on the calendar, looking up an address and listening to music—we love our smart phones.

Before waking up to the reality of slavery in the world, I used electronic devices without giving any thought about how they were made. I see phones differently now that I know about child soldiers: young boys ages six, seven, eight years old abducted from their families and given machine guns. These child soldiers are trained in brutal acts of rape and pillaging as a form of warfare.

Why are these kids trained to fight? To support rebel forces in certain African countries that are rich in the resources used to make cellular phones. Millions of people have been slaughtered, raped and displaced in conflicts over the mining of these minerals.

When I first learned about the horrific realities taking place in the Democratic Republic of Congo over the minerals used to make cell phones, I was tempted to give them up. But giving up our technologies will not solve the problems in DR Congo. We need to be thoughtful consumers but also work toward the manufacturing of products without the enslavement of children in parts of Africa.

The minerals used to make cell phones are located predominantly in the Democratic Republic of Congo, a beautiful and lush country in Africa plagued with what has been termed Africa's World War or the Great War of Africa. Corruption and violence are as abundant as its natural resources. The conflict in DR Congo was sparked by Rwandan genocide and Rwanda's subsequent invasion of DR Congo in 1996 and 1998. More than 5.4 million people have died as a result of mass murder, famine and disease born of the chaos, making it more deadly than World War II. Although the nation held peaceful elections in 2006, it was not enough to bring restoration to DR Congo's multilevel destruction, in which 45,000 people die each month and there is widespread displacement.

Yves Muya

Yves Muya was twelve years old when his family fled his beautiful country of DR Congo. "My favorite childhood memory was when our neighbors would come over for dinner on Sunday nights," Yves Muya shared with a room full of strangers in San Clemente. Yves recounted his childhood in the DR Congo with fondness—until he told of the rebels who came and scattered the people in his town.

"That day when we fled, my family went one way and our neighbors went the other," he said. "I just remember running and running." Yves and his family eventually made it to a refugee camp in Malawi where he spent his adolescent years.

"I was a growing boy and remember being hungry a lot then," Yves told us. "We had to stand in line for hours a day to get our food rations. I was lucky that I had my parents. My dad reminded me to dream. Many refugees forget how to dream. I was lucky that I did not forget how to dream. I think it is part of what kept me alive."

Between the ages of twelve and fifteen Yves's family lived in the refugee camp. His dad quickly saw that the only hope for their family was to somehow get out.

"I could not possibly imagine how I was going to live when my dad told us that we had to begin to ration half of our food," Yves continued. "I was already hungry all the time. How was I going to survive on half of what I was eating? My dad figured selling our food would be the only way our family would get the money to travel out of the refugee camp." For an entire year his family took half of their food ration and sold it to others. Eventually they had enough money to begin their journey out.

With a casualness and peace about him, Yves shared how the hardest part of that time in his life was walking to South Africa. Beginning in a refugee camp in Malawi, Yves and his family walked through Malawi, through Mozambique, through Zambia to the border of South Africa.

"Although I was scared at times of different militia groups, I was mostly scared of the wild animals that I knew were out where we were sleeping," he said with a large smile. "You know there are parts that are really wild in Africa."

He continued, "Yes, it was hard, but not as hard as my neighbors had it. While at the refugee camp, we heard our friends were captured and eventually killed by the militia group that came into our town that day. I don't know exactly how they died. I didn't want to know. I had already heard too much. We were the lucky ones."

After Yves's talk that night, those in attendance were sobered as we absorbed what he experienced as a teenager. As mothers we could not imagine what it would be like to watch our kids go hungry day after day and hope they would make it out alive. Eventually Yves's family made it to South Africa where they are still living today.

Through one blessed circumstance after another, this charismatic man eventually received a scholarship at Pitzer College in California and came to the United States to study. He volunteers his time speaking about his experience growing up in DR Congo in hopes of educating others and bringing peace to his homeland.

A World Away yet in My Home

DR Congo's abundant resources have been called "the curse of the Congo." The history of the country tells a story of invasion after invasion of foreign powers exploiting the resources and the Congolese people. Even though DR Congo is estimated to have more than $20 trillion in natural resources at its disposal, it is ranked last on the United Nations' human development report. This report is a standard of living assessment reflecting life expectancy, educational access, literacy, income and child welfare.[1] DR Congo is considered the top worst place in the world to be a woman today. Sexual violence committed by the armed militia groups is a way of life for Congolese women. It is estimated that 400,000 women are raped in DR Congo annually.

A top reason for continued violence in DR Congo is the mining of minerals. There are four main minerals mined in DR Congo: tin, tantalum, tungsten (often referred to as the three T's) and gold. Another name of tantalum is coltan, which is the essential semiconductor in all electronics, including aircraft engines and military equipment. Tungsten is the magic that makes our cell phones vibrate. Tin is used as a solder on circuit boards. Gold is in jewelry but is also used in electronics. These minerals eventually end up in every electronic product on the market.

Due to instability in DR Congo there are many different armed militia groups who use mass rape as a deliberate strategy to intimidate and control local people. The goal is to secure control of the mines and trading routes. Due to lack of transparency in the supply chain, electronics companies don't know where the minerals they use come from, whether areas of conflict or not. As consumers we have no way of knowing if we are inadvertently financing the armed groups forcing children to fight and who routinely commit mass rape. As we search on the Internet, text friends and listen to music on our surround-sound systems, men, women and children in DR Congo are forced to work for the minerals used to make our devices.

Recently there has been increased awareness and understanding of what is taking place in DR Congo, thanks to individuals and organizations who work alongside and on behalf of the Congolese people. There have been global discussions on how to find a solution. Recently legislation has been passed making supply chain transparency essential. Some argue it is too complicated to trace the supply of minerals, too expensive, and therefore too difficult to regulate. An article by Enough Project founders John Prendergast and Sasha Lezhenv is titled "From Mine to Mobile Phone: The

Conflict Mineral Supply Chain" and concludes that it is possible
for the supply chain of minerals to become transparent.

Here is the journey DR Congo minerals make from the mines to
our cell phones:

1. *The mines.* There are approximately two hundred mines in the
eastern part of DR Congo. The United Nations and the International Peace Information Service estimate that fifty percent of these
mines are controlled by a variety of armed groups. Each group controls the mines in its own way, but all mines have abysmal working
conditions with no health and safety standards. The armed groups
may compensate people minimally or work them as slaves. Most
armed groups controlling mines receive up to ninety percent of the
profits.

2. *Trading houses.* After they're mined from the earth, the minerals are loaded in sacks and shipped to two major cities in the
region, Bukavu and Goma.

3. *Exporters.* The minerals enter the international markets.
There are seventeen export companies based in Bukavu and
twenty-four in Goma. These companies must register with the government to buy minerals from the trading houses and transporters.
They then process the minerals and sell them to foreign buyers.
These companies are often paid in advance by international traders
from other countries.

4. *Transit countries.* Once the minerals have been processed, the
exporters send them to neighboring countries such as Rwanda,
Uganda and Burundi. Even though some of these minerals are le-
gally exported—meaning taxes are paid to the Congolese government—most are considered conflict minerals as to their point
of origin. Rarely if ever are questions asked about where the minerals were mined.

5. *Refiners.* Minerals are refined into metals and then sold on the
open world market. According to the Enough Project, the com-

panies involved are primarily in East Asia. "When it comes to tracing supply chains back to their sources, refiners are the critical link," because once the specific mineral is refined into metal, it becomes impossible to distinguish whether it came from DR Congo or another source country.[2]

6. *Electronics companies.* The final refined products are sold to electronic companies—the largest consumer of minerals from eastern DR Congo. The metals then become part of our computer chips, cell phones, MP3 players and notebooks.

Creating a system of transparency is a big factor in reducing violence and abolishing slavery in DR Congo. In 2010 the passage of the Dodd-Frank Wall Street Reform Act was an initial effort by the U.S. government to trace conflict minerals, reform supply chains and develop auditing protocols. Today, companies that manufacture products requiring tin, tantalum, tungsten and gold must report where the minerals originated. If minerals originate in DR Congo or neighboring countries, the companies must file a report describing the measures taken to understand where and how the minerals were acquired.

Although this legislation is far from a silver bullet, it does begin to move our country in the right direction: taking profits out of the hands of the armed militia groups and building a system of ethical trading, resulting in profits to the Congolese people. This is a big undertaking, but some companies are responding. Apple was the first major electronics company to completely map its supply chain in order to trace the materials used in its products back to their source.[3]

Even though most minerals come out of the soil of another continent, they are in our homes, in our pockets or adorning our fingers. This is the global economy in which we live. As consumers we play a large role in asking questions and reminding companies that we care about this issue. We must communicate that slave labor, rape and terror of any kind is unacceptable in the supply chain of our electronic products. We need to put pressure on companies to monitor their supply chains and stay involved in the solution.

One way to stay directly involved is to follow and participate in the actions of Raise Hope for Congo, a campaign of the Enough Project that aims to build a group of supporters who will advocate for the citizens of DR Congo and work toward ending violence in the eastern part of the country. Raise Hope for Congo collaborates with national and local groups in the United States as well as local Congolese organizations. Its website, www.raisehopeforcongo.org, is a great resource for educating oneself on current issues, including the role that conflict minerals play in funding the ongoing violence and the effects of sexual violence used as a weapon of war.

Through its partnership with the Enough Project, the movement has created targeted policy recommendations for the U.S. government. Its advocates have also developed a company ranking system to educate consumers, empowering them to make purchasing decisions regarding conflict minerals. Through the website one can take action to directly advocate on behalf of the Congolese people. For example, in less than five minutes one can directly send letters to eighteen electronics companies asking them to produce conflict-free electronics.

LRA, Invisible Children and Mothers

Groups such as the Lord's Resistance Army, the Democratic Forces for the Liberation of Rwanda, and Mai Mai are some of the worst perpetrators of sexual violence against women and children in history. Cases of group rape—up to fifty women in one village—are common as these groups attempt to control different territories. Few cases are ever brought to trial, there is no justice for victims, and the groups continue their terror with impunity.[4]

The Lord's Resistance Army is of particular concern. They don't claim to fight for anything but simply exist to terrorize. Joseph

Kony is the self-appointed leader and has abducted thousands of children to fight in his army beginning in 1987; originally he operated in northern Uganda. Eventually the LRA was pushed out of Uganda but continued its terror in DR Congo, Central African Republic and South Sudan.

Kony's tactics are savage and brutal. When he abducts children, he often forces them to kill their parents to indoctrinate them into his rebel cult. Children make up approximately ninety percent of the LRA soldiers with well over thirty thousand children abducted since Kony's beginnings in the late eighties. These children are forced to become soldiers, to work as porters, or to be "wives" or sex slaves of the senior officers.[5]

Shannon Sedgwick Davis, mother of two and CEO of the Bridgeway Foundation, visits Central Africa regularly and has seen firsthand the results of the extreme sexual violence perpetuated by these groups. The goal of the Bridgeway Foundation is to be a catalyst for hope and reconciliation throughout the world. "Our goal is a world without genocide," she explains. Lately her primary focus has been on the arrest of LRA commanders such as Kony and ending the war in Central Africa.

The violence toward women in these regions is absolutely staggering. "Even if we had real time accurate statistics informing us of the women who are raped, held as slaves, and killed we would still be understating this issue," Shannon explains. "Kony has set the bar for evil. He blindfolds little boys and makes them shove guns up their moms' vaginas and pull the trigger. Then he takes the blindfolds off and makes them look at the destruction."[6] This extreme sexual violence has caught the attention of actor Ben Affleck, who recently founded the Eastern Congo Initiative working with and on behalf the Congolese people, of which Shannon is a board member.[7]

In 2003 three college students began documenting the lives of young children who commuted into the center of a larger city in

Uganda each night afraid of being abducted by the LRA. Listening to the night commuters share stories of abductions and murder in their villages, the college students first began to learn about the terror of Joseph Kony and the Lord's Resistance Army.

Three years later Bridgeway Foundation funded its first film project, resulting in thousands of people being informed about the lives of the child night commuters in Uganda. As these college students grew into men, they were more determined than ever to put an end to the suffering caused directly by the purposeless violence of the LRA. In 2006 Invisible Children became an official nonprofit organization.

Invisible Children works to raise awareness of the violent realities in the region where the LRA is active, raises funds for on-the-ground projects that protect the Congolese people, and supports local Congolese people in bringing justice, healing and hope to their communities.

Through its films, Invisible Children began a movement of thousands of college students across the United States, educating and mobilizing them to action. The LRA and Joseph Kony are still active and acting with impunity. In 2012 Invisible Children launched a mass awareness campaign about Kony in order to apply global public pressure, making his arrest a priority. Invisible Children was not alone in its passionate plea to end LRA violence and to stop Kony and other violent leaders once and for all.

Many organizations and individuals have been tirelessly working both locally and internationally to put pressure on influential leaders and organize a united plan to put an end to LRA terror. Yet it was Invisible Children's twenty-seven-minute Kony video in 2012 that exceeded all expectations and broke viewership records, with more than 100 million views in less than two weeks. No one could have predicted the attention the campaign received. This incredible success brought the organization both wanted and unwanted attention as well as praise and criticism.[8]

As this book is being finalized, the outcome of the campaign is yet to be determined. What we do know is that Invisible Children has been an integral partner in working against violence with numerous well-respected organizations in Uganda and DR Congo for more than ten years. Its members are regarded as humble, smart, passionate and committed to both local people and those they work with. As Theodore Roosevelt said,

> It is not the critic who counts; not the man who points out how the strong man stumbles, or where the doer of deeds could have done them better. The credit belongs to the man who is actually in the arena, whose face is marred by dust and sweat and blood, who strives valiantly; who errs and comes short again and again; because there is not effort without error and shortcomings; but who does actually strive to do the deed; who knows the great enthusiasm, the great devotion, who spends himself in a worthy cause, who at the best knows in the end the triumph of high achievement and who at the worst, if he fails, at least he fails while daring greatly. So that his place shall never be with those cold and timid souls who know neither victory nor defeat.[9]

Much of the criticism of Invisible Children's Kony 2012 campaign came from the sidelines, from people who were concerned about the methods used in the appeal to action and how the organization was structured. However, most of the critics were not directly engaged in the fight against slavery in DR Congo themselves. Whatever concerns one may have about their methods, these young men did not resume "life as usual" after witnessing the horrible injustices committed by the LRA. Instead they refused to do nothing, using their God-given gifts on behalf of the voiceless, the marginalized, the terrorized and the enslaved who live on the other side of the world. And in doing so they earned the respect of others who spend their lives working toward peace and prosperity for the beautiful people of the DR Congo. Shannon Sedgwick Davis writes on her blog, "I cannot speak highly enough of Invisible Children, or its young leaders, who have boldly enlisted thousands of people to end the war in Central Africa."[10]

Invisible Children often partners with experts such as Resolve Uganda, Enough Project and the Bridgeway Foundation, resulting in a comprehensive strategy to protect the most vulnerable in the regions terrorized by the LRA. One such on-ground collaboration has been the installation of radio towers in the region. These radio towers link communities currently affected by LRA violence. The radio towers provide a network to help warn communities of pending LRA attacks, and they allow local humanitarian groups to provide timely assistance to those in need. This network also feeds into the LRA Crisis Tracker, a public website that provides near-real-time information on current LRA activity.

Many child soldiers escape from the LRA but hide in the bush, afraid to return home because of potential reprisals for the atrocities they've been forced to commit. Some women of northern Uganda—widows, rape survivors and former abductees—have banded together to support one another and those orphaned by war and disease. These women sing, and the strength in their music inspired the Voice Project. The messages in these women's songs let former soldiers know they are forgiven and invite them to come home. The songs are passed by radio and word of mouth out into the bush, as far as the Sudan and DR Congo. And it's working. Former child soldiers are returning home.

Evil has reigned out in the open in Central Africa for far too long. Recently it has been exposed. As mothers we are angry at the evil that has been unleashed on the most vulnerable—children. Our hearts ache for the mothers in Central Africa who have little power to protect their own children. Davis writes,

> I am all too aware of the gulf that exist between my home in
> San Antonio and the villages of Central Africa. I have wept
> with mothers who cannot provide the most basic of human
> needs for their children, like shelter and safety. When I hear
> their stories, hold their children, I cannot help but think of
> my two sons in Texas. I am deeply discontented with a world
> where my boys can play games on an iPod while our brothers
> and sisters in Central Africa suffer and die at the hand of such
> evil. How does one reconcile these things? I look at my two
> sons and think about the gravity of love I have for them and
> know that the mothers in the wretched refugee camps care
> equally for their children and are forced to watch their
> children suffer under such terrible conditions.[11]

Reconciling these things is what sustains and fuels Davis's focus to
return and press forward in working toward peace in DR Congo
and surrounding countries. When she is gone, she misses her
children, but knows she is uniquely gifted and called to her work
and is reassured with the community of support given to her family
when she travels.

Many stories coming out of DR Congo we can hardly stomach.
Stories of faces being mutilated, bodies deteriorating after years of
slavery in mines, children forced to witness the rape of their
mothers are almost too much to hear but we must. Despite the
distance and the graphic stories of violence, these are fellow human
beings created in the image of God.

Bringing peace in the DR Congo has not been and will not be
easy. But this must not surprise us. The road to peace and justice
has never been an easy one. Patience, perseverance and unwav-
ering determination to bring freedom to all people is the mindset
we need. Freedom comes only when people refuse to do nothing

and get to work. Whether it be contacting our favorite electronics companies to let them know we will support companies that actively pursue a slave-free supply chain or fundraising for organizations that are on the ground protecting and tirelessly working for peace in DR Congo, there is something each one of us can do.

Lisa Shannon and Thousand Sisters

In 2005, after watching an episode of *Oprah* and learning that millions had died in Congo and that rape and torture were occurring in shocking numbers, Lisa Shannon ran a solo thirty-mile run to sponsor Congolese women through Women for Women International. Her run launched Run for Congo Women, the first national grassroots effort for women in Congo, which to date has raised more than $11 million through events and media appearances and directly aided more than 66,000 Congolese women and children. What I love about her grassroots organization, Thousand Sisters, is that it focuses on two things: personal action and policy work. There are opportunities to raise funds through running as well as to stay connected with other women in Congo through letter writing. The website athousandsisters .org is an excellent resource to get you started.

Reflect

1. Put yourself in the place of a mother of a child soldier. What would you want?

2. What are your thoughts and emotions about the atrocities in DR Congo? What can you do to help?

Take Action

1. Raise Hope For Congo provides consumers with an easy tool. Email your favorite electronics company and ask questions about its supply chain. Ask if its minerals are conflict-free. Visit raisehopeforcongo.org. In less than two minutes you can tell Apple, IBM, Intel, HP and seventeen other electronics companies that they should care about the people in DR Congo.

2. Support Invisible Children's efforts either through screening one of their films, buying a T-shirt or making a monthly donation.

3. Visit freetheslaves.net to learn more about the problem of conflict minerals and ways you can support solutions.

Chocolate, Not So Sweet

Shayne Moore

There's slavery in every shopping mall in America.
From cocoa, coffee and clothing, to cars, computers and cell phones—
many products sold in the U.S. are tainted by slavery. Sometimes it's
sweatshop slavery where goods are manufactured. Other times,
it's brutal child slavery at plantations and mines where
commodities and raw materials come from.

FREETHESLAVES.NET

Miriam is from Sagu, a village in the poverty-stricken nation of Mali, in West Africa. When we meet Miriam she is reserved, quiet, maybe even embarrassed. Miriam has been rescued by some vigilant and caring men from a bus crossing into the Ivory Coast. She was being smuggled across the border and was to be sold into slavery to work on a cocoa plantation in the Ivory Coast.

Miriam was not alone on the bus. Rather she was escorted by a trafficker—an elusive woman who disappeared as authorities closed in on the scene. We don't know how Miriam knew the woman. Did the trafficker come to Miriam's village promising her parents work for their daughter—essential income for the family to survive? What was Miriam's life such that a mother and a father would agree to give a stranger their child in the hopes of some income?

When Miriam is rescued at the bus station, the hub for trafficking children from Mali into the Ivory Coast, she is shy and even looks disappointed and worried at being rescued, at the sudden change of plans. Poverty is a powerful motivator and the fuel feeding modern-day slavery. We learn that Miriam is twelve years old. When asked if she misses her family she replies, yes. But she admits that if she goes home to her family without money they will be angry.

We know Miriam because we see her real-life story unfold in front of us in Miki Mistrati's revealing documentary, *The Dark Side of Chocolate*. In this film, Mistrati claims that the trafficking of children into the Ivory Coast to work on cocoa plantations is "prevalent." Using hidden cameras, Mistrati and his crew unveil the obvious truth that the trafficking of children from Mali and other surrounding countries into the Ivory Coast to be used as labor on the cocoa plantations is a very real and accepted part of life on the border.

What compelled this Danish journalist to risk the dangers of making this film? What does this have to do with us on the other side of the world?

Did you know that the world consumes three million tons of chocolate every year? Half of that is consumed in Europe alone. Did you know that half of the world's cocoa, which is ultimately manufactured into our chocolate products, is grown in one country? It's the Ivory Coast.[1]

The chocolate industry has grown over the years, and in West Africa (where the Ivory Coast is located) cocoa is the commodity grown for export. Seventy percent of the world's cocoa is supplied by West African countries.[2] Yet the small plantation owner faces many struggles to make a profit. Governments are corrupt and often tax cocoa growers up to 35 percent of their harvest. These farmers barely make a living selling their cocoa beans and often resort to the use of child labor in order to keep their prices competitive.

Some children may work alongside their parents on these plantations making small pay or getting food and lodging, but many children are sold by their relatives to traffickers in the hopes of having income sent home. There are documented stories of traffickers abducting young boys from rural villages in neighboring countries such as Burkina Faso and Mali and transporting them to the Ivory Coast.[3]

Perhaps you have begun to hear inklings of this issue. In January 2012, Hershey's made the landmark announcement that it was going to expand its Responsible Cocoa Community Programs in West Africa. It pledged $10 million to programs such as CocoaLink, a program that uses SMS text messages to connect farmers with important information about improving farming practices, farm safety, child labor, health, crop disease prevention, post-harvest production and crop marketing. Hershey's also established the Hershey's Learn to Grow farm program in Ghana to help farmers learn best practices in cocoa farming, and it launched a new product, Bliss, that contains 100 percent cocoa from Rainforest Alliance-certified farms.[4]

But still, why are we just now hearing about the need for these initiatives against child labor and child slavery on cocoa farms?

In 2001 reports surfaced about human trafficking and child labor perpetrated by individuals within the chocolate industry. Consumers were outraged to discover that child labor, child trafficking and other human rights abuses existed on the cocoa farms of the Ivory Coast, a nation that produces over half of the world's chocolate. At that time, it has been reported that an "avalanche of negative publicity and consumer demands for answers and solutions followed."[5]

Two members of Congress, Senator Tom Harkin of Iowa and

Representative Eliot Engel of New York, responded to the cries and proposed an addition to an agriculture bill that would require a federal system to certify and label chocolate products as "slave-free." This may seem boring, but it is significant. The fact that world leaders on another continent responded to their citizens' outrage as consumers of West African cocoa is no small thing.

In today's global village we live in complicated networks of interdependence. We all affect one another. What is grown on a small farm in West Africa is cut, packed and shipped to a city in the Ivory Coast where it is processed and bought and sold. The crop is then loaded on freight ocean liners and shipped to plants primarily in the United States and Europe. It is in these factories where the chocolate products we love are created—candy bars, baking chocolate, hot chocolate, and on and on.

What these two Congressmen did was significant. They started a push to put real pressure on the largest companies that buy cocoa from the small farms accused of child slavery and that then manufacture chocolate and make billions of dollars a year in revenue worldwide. The measure passed the House of Representatives, and the leading chocolate manufacturers sprung to action. The top companies, Cargill, Mars, Hershey's, Nestle, Barry Callebaut, and Saf-Cacao fought the legislation that would require them to label their products with "no child labor." Many products would not have fit the requirements for the labeling.

In 2001 these companies worked with legislators and agreed to a voluntary protocol to end the use of children as labor on cocoa plantations by 2005. It is reported that in 2005 the industry had failed to comply with the protocol terms and so a new deadline of 2008 was established. Again, the chocolate industry failed to eliminate child slavery and child labor on West African cocoa farms, the world's largest cocoa producer, and so a new deadline was set for 2010.[6]

Miki Mistrati's film *The Dark Side of Chocolate* is a response to a decade of little change in the trafficking and use of child slaves despite the creation of the Harkin-Engle Protocol. Mistrati and his crew take us to Mali, a poverty-stricken nation next to the Ivory Coast, with little or no export. We learn that traffickers go to rural and poor villages and lure away children. Some accusations exist that traffickers from the plantations come to the village market and take the children "without telling the parent."

We watch in horror as children are openly loaded on busses at the local bus stop and transported to a border town. Here the children are taken off the bus and then put on the back of motorcycles to be moved across the border undetected along back roads.

It is shocking and depressing to witness the number of adults it takes to traffic just one child. It is clear after watching this film that not only is the trafficking of children across the border from Mali to the Ivory Coast prevalent, it is ignored and accepted, if not endorsed, by the community in which it happens.

There is one glimpse of a compassionate man who lives on the border and who works tirelessly to rescue children. He is heartbroken and discouraged, explaining that he sees the trafficking of children every day of his life: "The situation to me today is very very sad and is heartbreaking to me. My life is full of these kind of situations and it is why I feel very very bad and cry."

Yet most of the characters we see accept trafficking as a form of business. It is simply what is done. The use of young children aged ten to fourteen as labor on farms where they receive no pay, have no parents, receive no education and eat little food is considered an acceptable business practice.

At a local union for the bus drivers who transport the trafficked children we are told, "The trafficking of children has always existed. The children are constantly leaving from the bus station. The children who are going to the Ivory Coast are twelve to fourteen years of age. The girls are eleven to twelve years old."

One trafficker admits he smuggles twelve to fifteen children at a time, explaining that there is a place in the Ivory Coast where the children are kept and sold to farmers in the area. The trafficked children generally come from rural areas. Traffickers take them to the border and then use motorcycles, which can maneuver on the back roads, to bring the children across the border.

The most chilling character is a young, handsome, smiling man. He does not look like an evil criminal. He does not look like a slave trader, whatever I thought that might look like. Smiling and at ease he explains, "You can't pin trafficking on the border on one person. One person takes them to the border, another takes them across and a third person receives them. It's not one person in particular. If people on the border say they don't traffic children, they're lying. The plantation owners pay us to take children across the border. I take several across."

It is clear in the film that poverty fuels the trafficking of children. The families need money, the traffickers need money, the plantation owners need money—this reality creates an acceptable culture of slavery and young victims. These children will not receive an education. Most of them will never get paid. Many will be beaten if they work slow or try to escape. The children are exposed to dangerous pesticides daily and almost all of them have scars on their bodies from wielding the dangerous machetes used to cut down the cocoa pods. All of these circumstances are clear violations of child labor standards set forth by the International Labor Organization. Depriving these children of a healthy life will have short-term and long-term effects on their lives, their countries and our world. The children working on cocoa farms have little hope of ever breaking the cycle of poverty.

It is difficult to think that the chocolate we enjoy every day, the sweet we consider a treat and comfort food, may have been harvested by slaves and produced by a system that knows child labor exists and seems to not care. Little has changed in the decade the spotlight has been on this issue. One child slave who escaped shares that he has never even tasted chocolate. When asked what he would say to people who eat chocolate made from slave labor, he replies, "People enjoyed something I suffered to make. When people eat chocolate, they are eating my flesh."[7]

The question remains: what can be done? If international labor laws, U.S. legislation, agreed-upon protocols for industry standards, local governments and police have not been willing or able to stop the problem, what are we to do as ordinary consumers?

Do we simply remain victims, or are we even conspirators, of child trafficking and child labor whenever we indulge in chocolate? Do we throw our arms up in defeat and refuse to buy or eat chocolate? Do we boycott Hershey's and Nestle? Do we deprive our children of Halloween candy?

There is an alternative, albeit controversial idea—fair trade. Fair trade is defined as "a system of exchange that honors producers, communities, consumers, and the environment. It is a model for the global economy rooted in people-to-people connections, justice, and sustainability."[8]

Fair trade chocolate and other products have begun to take a more prominent role on our grocery shelves and in the consumer's conscience. Fair trade labeling can be seen on coffee, chocolate and many other products. Any product labeled "fair trade" must undergo an independent third-party certification process that assesses poverty, sustainability and empowerment of the workers in the world's poorest countries.

Those who are proponents of fair trade explain that when consumers buy fair trade products they can be assured of a set of standards regarding the product. When you make fair trade choices, you are supporting a fair price for products; you are investing in the people and in the communities where the product is grown or manufactured. Fair trade producers are committed to environmental sustainability and the economic empowerment of small-scale producers. Lastly, when you purchase fair trade products you are supporting fair labor conditions where, it is claimed, human rights and child labor laws are strictly enforced.

There is a debate raging regarding whether fair trade really does what it says it does. Those who criticize the system claim that little money reaches the developing world. Most fair trade products cost more than the competitors' price, and manufacturers say this money goes back to the producers. Some have offered studies showing this is not the case, that fair trade helps the rich and even harms the small farmers by creating an inefficient marketing system, corruption and overproduction.

Regardless of the controversy, many people support fair trade, saying that at this point it's the only tool consumers can use to vote with their dollars. The website, slavefreechocolate.org explains, "Simply, the principle behind the fair trade movement is to bring farmers and producers out of poverty by paying a higher price for goods or commodities. Along with higher price comes a coop system where the farmers and producers receive education and help so they can afford to fulfill the guidelines [to be labeled fair trade]. These guidelines include rules of labor practices, including the use of children."

Both sides of the debate acknowledge that fair trade is a flawed system. Even those who support it admit it's difficult to guarantee that any chocolate we consume has not involved the use of child or slave labor. Some go so far as to recommend avoiding any chocolate produced from Ghana or the Ivory Coast.

Nathan George is the founder and director of the organization Trade as One, which specializes in fair trade gifts and products. He believes fair trade seeks to transform the lives of poor producers in the developing world by enabling them to use their skills and resources to work their way out of poverty. "Our experience has been that the poor don't want handouts—they want jobs," he says. Working with farmers and producers in the developing world and partnering with churches in the United States, Trade as One spreads its message and mission.

In an article written with Lynne Hybels, Nathan George explains, "Trade as One believes that ongoing purchasing partnerships between fair trade companies and local churches could significantly contribute to a more just distribution of the world's abundance. Nearly 43 percent of Americans regularly attend church, creating an automatic constituency of almost 130 million people. What could happen if 130 million Christians embraced fair trade as a means of bringing good news to the poor and meaning to the rich?"

As we have discussed, the trans-Atlantic African slave trade abolitionist movement began in the hearts and minds of Christians in England and in the United States. They were deeply convicted about the evils of slavery even though it was legal and believed to be the backbone of the global economy at that time.

Despite the enormous odds our abolitionist brothers and sisters faced two hundred years ago, they remained persistent in their convictions. During this time there were products with slave-free labels. Abolitionists spread the word to buy only these. In fact, historian Adam Hochschild writes that abolitionists took it a step further—a step that shifted the African slave trade abolitionist movement from the moral and religious spheres to the economic, getting the movement the political attention it needed.

The abolitionists boycotted sugar produced on slave-run plantations. He explains, "Quietly but subversively, the boycott added a new dimension to British political life. At a time when only a small fraction of the population could vote, citizens took upon themselves the power to act when Parliament had not. . . . The boycott of sugar was radical. . . . It struck not just at the slave trade but at slavery itself. And finally, the boycott was largely put into effect by those who bought and cooked the family food: women."[9]

Nathan George admits that boycotting is a more complicated idea in today's world than it would have been two hundred years ago. Today the large companies that buy and manufacture chocolate do not own the farms. We have a more complex and interconnected system. Boycotting chocolate altogether may serve only to harm the small farmers and perpetuate poverty. Poverty fuels the abuses in child labor in the chocolate industry.

George is a proponent of a more responsible and reasonable response. He believes not only that purchasing fair trade helps ensure that we're buying ethically but that fair trade is a Christian response to poverty. He acknowledges that aid to developing and impoverished countries is necessary, but in the long run it is not aid that will lift nations out of poverty. Rather it is things like fair trade, which creates jobs and comes alongside the poor. George explains, "It is clear the Bible teaches not to condemn the rich but to invite the poor back into community. There were special protections built in to scripture to protect the widow, orphan and the poor—the gleaning laws. God made rules that forced the wealthy to recognize the presence and provide for the poor in their midst."[10]

The reality that child slave labor is involved in potentially seventy percent of the world's cocoa production is no small thing. It is a complicated issue and can seem difficult to wrap our heads and hearts around. How do we turn such a huge ship?

We turn it together.

Many people have their eye on this issue. We are not doing it alone. The website foodispower.org has a complete list of chocolate companies it recommends as slave-free. At tradeasone.org you can order Divine and Alter Ego products, the leading brands of slave-free chocolate.

Together we raise our awareness and our voices. We let the

chocolate companies know we are educated consumers and we care about issues of child slavery. These companies are under much scrutiny. When we tried to get an interview with a person from Hershey's, we were referred to a spokesperson who speaks on behalf of the industry. Below is the email response we received from Hershey's. You can decide if it was a satisfactory response.

Dear Shayne,

Thank you for your interest in The Hershey's Company and the issue of cocoa farming labor practices in West Africa. We care deeply about these important issues and work hard to ensure that our cocoa is responsibly sourced.

Solving these issues requires a broad range of programs and approaches by all stakeholders across our industry, government, development organizations and nonprofits. No one company or entity—or single approach—can effectively solve these issues.

I would like to refer you to Susan Smith at the National Confectioners Association who works with manufacturers across the confectionery industry and is well-versed on the broad range of programs and initiatives under way in West Africa and other cocoa growing regions. She can provide a more complete perspective on what the entire industry in doing in conjunction with other key stakeholders to address these issues.

Susan can be reached at:
susan.smith@candyusa.com
(202) 534-1440

Thanks again for contacting us, and I'm confident that Susan will provide you with useful information for your book.

Best regards,
Jeff King, Hershey's

Feel free to contact Susan yourself. Tell her Kim and Shayne sent you.

- The International Labour Organization estimates that between 56 million and 72 million African children work in agriculture, many on their own family farms. The seven largest cocoa-producing countries are Indonesia, Nigeria, Cameroon, Brazil, Ecuador, the Ivory Coast and Ghana. Those last two together account for nearly sixty percent of global cocoa production.[11]
- Estimates are that up to forty percent of cocoa is slave-grown.[12]
- The cocoa industry creates billions of dollars a year. The Ivory Coast produces nearly half of all the world's cocoa; West Africa collectively supplies nearly seventy percent of the world's cocoa.[13]

Reflect

1. How might putting pressure on and boycotting companies that produce products via slave labor stop the use of children as slaves in cocoa production?

2. Do you think slave-free chocolate on an industry-wide level is possible? Why or why not?

Take Action

1. Watch the documentary *The Dark Side of Chocolate*.

2. Research the stores in your area that carry fair trade and slave-free chocolate.

12

You Have Purchasing Power

Kimberly McOwen Yim

Can you imagine what would happen if the church in America
began seeing itself as the conscience of the free market? Can you imagine the
enormous blessing that it could pour out on the rest of the world simply by
deciding to ensure that justice and compassion are built into how the
products we need and use every day are sourced?

NATHAN GEORGE, *TRADE AS ONE*

"Hey, don't grab any chocolate!" I called to my kids through the open door of the church.

I was caught off guard when the volunteer at youth group told my kids to grab a few pieces of Halloween candy on their way out. It was the first week of October. I had yet to tell them about my new idea.

"No chocolate? Why? I'm taking chocolate." Malia defiantly grabbed a mini candy bar.

"What's this all about, Mom?" Malia asked. "I love chocolate!"

"You remember last year I didn't buy anything chocolate to pass out for Halloween? Remember we talked about how we learned that children may be used to pick the cocoa beans and to work as slaves in certain areas of the world that harvest cocoa—which is used to make our chocolate?"

"Yes," she said. I could tell she didn't like where this was going.

"I've learned Hershey's is the only company that hasn't done much to address the problem since knowing about it for over ten years. I decided this year as a family we will not only not buy Hershey's candy but we won't eat it either." I ended on a high tone, confident they would think this was a great idea too.

They both stopped in their tracks in the parking lot. "What?" And then both of my children started crying.

It was as if they'd received news that their beloved pet had died—and we don't even own a pet. My daughter was seriously crushed.

"Malia, it's not all chocolate." I tried to console her. "Only chocolate from Hershey's. We can't in good faith learn about this and not do anything. I know you understand."

Honestly, I tried to be sympathetic to my children's emotions but I was also a bit frustrated that they actually cried over chocolate. I still don't understand exactly what that was all about, but their reactions gave me encouragement. Regardless of whether I was right to give up Hershey's for that season, it turned out to be a good exercise in being willing to give up a little for what you believe is right.

By the time Halloween had come to an end all was well at the Yim household. The kids had piles of candy. My children and I boxed up the Hershey's candy we did receive and sent it back to Hershey's along with a note asking them to offer some fair trade options.

A month after sending our chocolate back to Hershey's we received a three-page letter from a consumer representative thanking us for sharing our concerns and explaining all they were doing to help remedy the problem within the cocoa supply chain. If they really were doing all the things they said, I wondered why they weren't telling their customers more about it.

Soon after our Hershey's activities the company announced it was launching a fair trade line of products. I like to think the actions of our family directly resulted in Hershey's announcement, but I think our voices were a part of a collective around the world.

From cars to clothes to food, every industry uses commodities tainted by slavery. Our hope is that other industries will follow the chocolate industry and provide solutions in abolishing slavery. When the presence of slavery was revealed in the production of pig iron in Brazil, Ford Motor Company suspended imports of Brazilian pig iron and began to investigate the problem. There are companies like Ford that care about the issue, yet there still needs to be more collaboration among industries. Are other car companies reaching out to Ford, asking them what they discovered about slave labor in the production of pig iron? No company supports slavery, but what are companies willing to risk to learn whether slavery is touching their supply chains? Will they be willing to share ideas with other companies to eradicate slavery in their industry?

It is also important that companies hear from their customers. Without that input, many will continue to make decisions based only on their bottom line. We, the consumers, are the last link in the supply chain. Therefore we have considerable power. "By speaking in one voice, consumers can bring enough pressure to bear to remove the slavery ingredient from the things we buy," writes Kevin Bales, president of Free the Slaves.[1] As consumers we can begin to ask our favorite companies what they are doing to be part of the solution in becoming a slave-free economy. We can ask them to partner with anti-slavery organizations and to be transparent in their supply chains.

When making the film *Call + Response* Justin Dillon impulsively shot Steve Jobs an email asking him if he knew whether the tantalum used to make the iPhone was mined using slave labor. Jobs replied, "I have no idea. I'll look into it."[2]

Apple's honest and nondefensive response has led the company to now be a leader in creating a slave-free economy. Apple took the lead in 2010 by hiring a third-party auditor to trace its supply chain and publicly releasing the findings. By 2011 Apple, along with Intel, had made a conscious decision to buy conflict-free minerals, which has resulted in their looking for buyers in Asia.[3] In 2012 Apple announced it would become the first fair trade technology company.[4]

Dillon's voice was one among many putting pressure on Apple to be transparent in its supply chain. As more and more electronics companies begin to join with Apple and Intel in addressing the problem of slave labor in their supply chains, we the consumers must continue to thank them for facing this complicated issue head-on. We put our purchasing power to work by putting pressure on our favorite companies to provide slave-free products.

Locked in tiny sheds, fed very little and forced to work long days without a chance of education, child slaves have been producing hand-woven rugs in India, Pakistan and Nepal for years. Rugs made in these regions have been well-known to be tainted by slavery. Up until recently there was no way for consumers to know whether or not they were supporting the slavery of children with their purchases.

An organization called GoodWeave began with the intention of providing inspection and licensing to protect children and guarantee slave-free products. GoodWeave's founder, Kailash Satyarthi, spent many years rescuing Indian children from bonded labor in the carpet industry. These rescued children were simply replaced with other victims. He wanted to create a market incentive for manufacturers to stop exploiting children on an industry-wide basis. GoodWeave was formally established in 1994. Since then more than 7.5

million carpets have been sold through the GoodWeave program and are now found in Macy's department stores in the United States as well as other carpet and interior design businesses.

The mission of GoodWeave is to end exploitation of child labor in the carpet industry and to offer educational opportunities to children around the world. The organization works to fulfill its mission by making unannounced, independent inspections of factories and looms that wish to be compliant with GoodWeave certification. GoodWeave provides rehabilitation, counseling, education and a home for rescued child laborers and at-risk children. It helps build awareness of the plight of the world's "carpet kids" and the power consumers have to help them.[5] There are other certification labels, but only GoodWeave provides a third-party inspection in its certification process.

GoodWeave is a great example of how we as consumers can begin to question our favorite brands and show companies examples of what others in manufacturing and business are doing to address the concern of slavery in supply chains.

Many people claim that in our global economy it's too difficult to address the supply chain and to guarantee slave-free products. We believe that nothing is too hard or justifies the enslavement of other human beings. It might be challenging, but it is not impossible. There are industries and companies that have trailblazed the way in ethical production and are continually working toward a slave-free economy.

As consumers we have power. Companies spend millions of dollars in marketing strategies to get our attention and build a relationship with us in order to get us to buy their products. They create surveys, campaigns and advertisements all in hopes that their investment will pay out later in our exchange of money for their services or goods. We need to let them know we care whether men, women and children are enslaved to make the products we buy. We need to communicate to our favorite companies and brands that we will put our money toward those that are honestly and transparently working toward a slave-free economy.

In 2011 Justin Dillon, with a grant from the U.S. State Department, worked to create a computer-based platform that would aid consumers in electronically communicating their desires for slave-free products to their favorite companies. Almost 150 years after President Lincoln issued the Emancipation Proclamation, Slavery Footprint was released.

This platform is similar to the idea behind a carbon footprint. It calculates approximately how many slaves you as a consumer have working for you based on your lifestyle and purchases. It puts you in touch with the brands you use and gives you an easy tool to communicate with the companies.

You can link to Slavery Footprint at slaveryfootprint.org or via a mobile app called FreeWorld. After you take a brief survey your slavery footprint is calculated. Now you can begin to improve your footprint by contacting your favorite brands, asking companies for products not tainted by slavery and asking the same companies to monitor their supply chains.

What we like about Slavery Footprint is how simple it is to use. You can draft your own letter or use a provided template. From A&W root beer to Zyrtec, you can tell your favorite brands that this issue is important to you and ask them to be a part of the solution.

The goal of Slavery Footprint is to gather market research, give consumers direct access to their favorite brands to make their request for slave-free products, and communicate to companies that it's in their best interest to move away from slave labor and monitor their supply chains.

In less than five minutes, while out to eat at our favorite pizza place, we check in using the app. We then send a letter to the owner of the pizza chain, the company that produces the cheese on the pizza, and the owner of the winery that produces the wine we're enjoying and communicate that we care about living in a free world. By using this app we ask companies what they are doing to ensure slavery isn't in their products. That is leveraged consumer power.

Being an educated and informed consumer is important to my friends and me.

During one of our meetings Julie, another Abolitionist Mama, told us about a fashion show in our area that was supporting anti–human trafficking efforts. She didn't know much about it, but tickets were only twenty dollars, and Sandra Morgan, the director of the Orange County Human Trafficking Task Force, would be speaking.

It was local and within our budget. We were in. The five of us met early for dinner and headed to a large warehouse in a business park in Irvine, California, where we attended the Freedom and Fashion show.

Freedom and Fashion was started by Bonnie Kim after she volunteered at Nightlight, an organization fighting human trafficking in Bangkok, Thailand. After learning about the number of organizations working on the front lines to fight human trafficking, Bonnie realized that these groups needed ongoing financial support.

After much prayer, she decided to use her passion for art and fashion for social justice and to create a platform for organizations working to combat modern-day slavery. Focusing on fair trade and other cause-oriented collections, Freedom and Fashion is a fashion and creative arts ministry that "serves as a resource hub for fair trade businesses and non-profit organizations working to combat modern-day slavery, human trafficking, child labor and human rights violations."[6]

With more than eight hundred people—mostly young college students—in attendance, Freedom and Fashion hosted its first fashion show. That evening not only exposed us to new organizations, it launched our effort to educate others about the real purchasing power we have and gave us practical ways we could redirect our spending.

For instance, this was where we first learned about Krochet Kids. Krochet Kids sells hats. Each hat is handmade and signed by a woman in Uganda who is working to build a better life for her family. From the tag on the hat you can go online and learn about the exact woman who made your hat and send her a note of thanks.

The story of Krochet Kids is even more interesting when you learn that it wasn't founded by grandmas but rather three young men who love to crochet. After his brother taught him to crochet, cofounder Kohl Crecelius taught his two friends to do the same. Still in high school, these three snowboarding friends began to make their own headgear and eventually were named Krochet Kids by a local reporter who highlighted them in an article.

While in college, the boys took trips to developing nations to be exposed to the needs of the world and realized how fortunate they were to live in the United States. One trip to Uganda inspired them. While in Uganda they learned about entire communities living in government camps for more than twenty years because a rebel militia group had destroyed much of the northern part of their country. After years of relying on government support for their basic needs, these Ugandan people were tired of dependence and wanted opportunities to provide for their own families.

With hooks and yarn the boys sat and taught a small group of women how to crochet. In 2008 they officially became a nonprofit organization that now employs more than 150 people in both Uganda and Peru. Each hat is signed by the person who made it and items are sold both online and in some retail stores.

Nine months after learning about Krochet Kids at the Freedom and Fashion show, I was thrilled when I saw their hats at Nordstrom. That year all the Abolitionist Mamas purchased Krochet Kids hats for our Christmas gifts. It felt very satisfying to know we were coming alongside people in need in Uganda and making a difference. We were also able to share the story and message of Krochet Kids and life in Uganda through the giving of the hats. This gift helps to raise a family out of poverty on the other side of the world.

I don't know about you, but I like to find a good deal. Often when people compliment me on what I'm wearing, I reply with "Thanks!" and then go into the backstory of what a great deal it was. Why is it when I buy something nice that's inexpensive I think

Our favorite places to redirect our spending

- *Trade As One (tradeasone.com).* Great fair trade rice, olive oil and chocolate-covered bananas. We love their bag of the month.

- *Riji Green (rijigreen.com).* Looking for a place to buy great-quality bags with your own custom logos? Great selection.

- *Punjammies (punjammies.com).* Pajamas and loungewear made by women in India who have been rescued from sex trafficking. Proceeds from the sales provide fair wages, savings accounts and holistic recovery care to the women.

- *Isanctuary (isanctuary.org).* Jewelry made by survivors of sex trafficking in India and the United States. Survivors are paid a fair wage and given rehabilitation options. They also work both domestically and internationally on a number of prevention programs.

- *Laugh Brand (laughbrand.com).* Ethically made children's clothing. Thirty percent profits go to fighting child sex trafficking.

I'm a smart shopper?

Recently I have been convicted by my "cheap is better" mentality. I will always want a good value, but now I pause at the point of purchase and ask questions. "Why is this so cheap? I wonder if the person who made this was paid a fair wage?"

Unlike slavery in the past, where slave-made goods were common and made up the majority of the marketplace, modern-day slavery is a much smaller fraction tainting almost all commodities and products. Our global economy has created a marketplace for cheap labor, and although slavery has been documented in nearly all types production of consumable goods, it is still very difficult to identify and therefore eliminate. From clothes to cars to food, slavery has touched our lives.

- *Nomi Network (buyherbagnotherbody.com).* I purchased a laptop case from these folks at a World Vision event. Love it and their message.

- *Krochet Kids (krochetkids.org).* You can also look for their goods at Nordstrom. A few local surf shops in my hometown carry them as well.

- *Raven and Lily (ravenandlily.com).* I love the jewelry from their Ethiopia line, where beads and charms are made from melted bullet castings.

- *Beza Threads (bezathreads.org).* Buy a scarf and keep a child out of sex trafficking in Ethiopia.

- *Freeset (freesetglobal.com).* Fair trade business offering employment to women trapped in Kolkata's sex trade.

- *4the1 (4the1.org).* Through the selling fair trade products, 4the1 funds both local and international anti-human trafficking projects and shelters.

I may not get the answers right away but now I'm asking questions. And sometimes I find myself putting things down and simply not buying them. I am changing the way I consume. Once we realize the greater picture of modern-day slavery and understand our purchasing power, we must ask ourselves, "What we are going to do with our power?"

With power comes responsibility. I have come to believe that when it comes to my purchasing power, I begin with prayer for wisdom. This is countercultural thinking in a world where impulse buying and the "we want what we want" mentality is embedded in our consuming habit. In slowing down, thoughtfully questioning how things are made and produced, we will be able to reallocate our spending to slave-free items that we need and begin to understand what a real value is: when all lives are treated with dignity.

"Mom, did you see that The Cellar has the dark peppermint chocolate we like?" my daughter asked.

"Yes. Dawn told me they were getting some in this year for Christmas," I replied.

The Cellar, where my San Clemente abolitionist friends meet, is also where the best selection of fair trade chocolate bars can be found in a forty-mile radius. I love it when you can support both local business and fair trade.

"Can we get one? Maybe two? I think Grandpa would love it!" Malia asked excitedly.

Since my chocolate prohibition at Halloween I had made it up to Malia by buying her some really good specialty fair trade chocolate. She was now becoming a chocolate connoisseur. I'm not sure if these candy bars are her all-time favorite, but she is learning to ask the right questions when it comes to chocolate.

"Why don't we get four bars and give them as teachers' gifts this year?"

"Awesome idea, Mom."

Reflect

1. In what ways do your purchases have power?

2. Whta would it take to begin to change your consumer habits? What are your concerns?

3. What are some of the obstacles you see in creating a slave-free economy?

Take Action

1. Go to Slavery Footprint at slaveryfootprint.org and download the FreeWorld application.

2. Convert a small percentage of your essential consumer spending to fair trade through Trade as One's Change for Good program. This program sends a hamper four times a year to your doorstep—rice, olive oil, chocolate, coffee, soaps, couscous, tea, you name it. You get to learn the stories behind the products, and besides providing dignified jobs to the people who make the products, you also send seeds that feed a family their vegetables for a whole year. It's an incredibly easy way to build justice into your regular spending.

3. Challenge a small group or church that you're part of to participate in Trade as One's Hungry for Change program. Eat in solidarity with those on two dollars a day for five days. Figure out how much you have saved in that period and give it away to a group project to change the lives of the poor. The program guides you through daily reflection from a majority world theologian, provides you with the product to eat (rice, beans and oatmeal) and gives you instructions on how to do the challenge.

13

You Have Relationship Power

Shayne Moore

*What makes women's relationships powerful
is our natural bent toward win-win, consensus building,
and ensuring the inclusion of others. In our globally connected
world women are natural change agents—whether in local community
development where helping one woman impacts an entire community,
to leading civil society, or at the peace table in conflict.*

CINDY BREIHL, WORLD VISION

Saving the world in a chocolate and wine restaurant? Yes, please.
Although Carrie and I had attended a bit of college together, it took twenty years and a justice conference—along with some chocolate and wine—to bring us together. I was in Bend, Oregon, speaking at World Relief's first-ever Justice Conference. My message resonated with Carrie, and so an invitation to a trendy chocolate and wine spot in the city reconnected us.

When like-minded women find one another, the flow of conversation, energy, ideas and connection is an awesome thing to experience. I was just beginning my journey into understanding the reality of modern-day slavery. Carrie's heart was broken by it and she had a dream. A plan.

You see, what broke her heart also sparked her creative imagination. She reached into her own life for solutions to the problem of modern-day slavery. Slowly sipping wine I listened to her tale like a little girl opening a present—delighted. Carrie's story is about her relationship with God, herself, those close to her, and the world at large. Her story is similar to ours; but as only God can orchestrate it, it is also unique.

> I first discovered what I wanted to do with my life in 1990 while attending a social activism conference in Philadelphia. Back then the term "social justice" was not used much— especially in the Christian culture. I was not familiar with it but this conference and these ideas sparked something within me. I have a clear memory of standing at the window in a building we converted from a crack house to a family home with Habitat for Humanity. Filled with the joy of the experience and the reality of what we accomplished I blurted out, "I think I could do this for a living!"
>
> Thankfully God knew what I needed as I began to live out his calling on my life. I have learned to surround myself with close friends and like-minded people. When fighting injustice in the world we cannot do it alone. We need the support of loving people.
>
> Ever since my first encounter with living out my faith in a tangible way in Philadelphia, I knew how important it was for me to be in a mentorship relationship. I thank my mom for instilling this in me at a young age. Ever since Philly I have had a mentor in my life—a woman who is older, wiser, one who speaks truth into every area of my life.
>
> My mentorship relationships have played an integral role

when I get discouraged and when naysayers cause me to doubt myself and what I am called to do. When the road-blocks and critical voices start to take a toll on me I look to my mentor to help me sift through it and discard what is destructive. These relationships help me see what I need to learn from tough situations. I seek to always grow and learn in order to become more of what God intends for me. Today I believe if I have done anything well or been successful I owe much of it to these relationships. I listen to my mentors and I trust God is speaking through them.

I have also learned the importance of authentic collaboration. This has been an area of intention for me. I chose to go to Eastern University for graduate school because I knew I would find kindred spirits and I knew I would be encouraged to live out my passions in activism. I made lifelong friends while at Eastern and I now have a phenomenal network of like-minded friends throughout the world.

The inception of my organization, Someone's Child, came about in a very organic way. I first heard a trafficking story from one of my students while teaching in the Czech Republic in the mid 1990s. At that time I had no frame of reference to identify that what I was hearing was an incident of modern-day slavery. However, her story stirred something in me—a strong desire to see the injustice of it made right.

I taught at-risk high school students for a decade. Many of my students were from migrant worker families. My kids would miss school in order to work in the fields. I had students who came from gang families and were involved with gangs. I loved working with these kids—"my kids"—and my relationship with them fortified my heart to work toward fighting these connected injustices. What I learned from my students and the reality of their lives continues to inform my desire to eradicate all forms of slavery.

One weekend a few years ago my husband and I saw a powerful movie on modern-day slavery. There was a panel discussion where we learned how to define and understand this new epidemic called human trafficking. The same weekend, we saw *Slumdog Millionaire*—again our hearts were completely broken over this issue.

Soon after seeing *Call + Response* we traveled to Ethiopia to bring home our adopted daughter. While in Ethiopia I visited a friend who runs a rehabilitative shelter for former prostitutes. I saw trafficked victims firsthand, learned about their experiences and the profound hope available to these women through rescue, rehabilitation and career training.

That visit changed me forever. I became an abolitionist— but I was not sure what this would look like in my life.

The more I hosted events in my home and volunteered for anti-trafficking organizations, the more I began to realize how difficult it was to engage women like me—everyday full-time moms. One night after an event I was talking with a group of friends, all moms, about this missing and frustrating piece.

"Carrie, have you ever thought of starting an anti-trafficking organization specifically to engage moms?" asked my longtime friend.

I looked at her blankly. Despite all my years of experience, all my passion, knowledge and expertise, I had never thought of it. Like-minded people and friends who know you deeply help plumb the creative spaces in ways that change your life.

Someone's Child was born. Some of the moms from that conversation became my cofounders. For the past year and a half we have grown faster than we can keep up with. We consistently receive encouragement and confirmation from others in the anti-trafficking movement that Someone's Child is meeting a need—engaging everyday women and moms and inviting them to join the fight, to become abolitionists.

This is integral to what we do at Someone's Child. We believe every mom has her own unique God-given gifting that can be used to combat global human trafficking. We get excited when we see a mom tap into her gifting and watch as she finds a unique and personal way to do her part.

When this happens there is a ripple effect in her sphere of influence. It is awesome to watch a woman transform the way her family, church and friends think about modern-day slavery as she raises awareness just by living out her life where she is.

Someone's Child partners with other anti-trafficking organizations in providing moms with tangible ways to engage. We wholeheartedly believe that if we are to be effective as an organization, we need to collaborate and build relationships with as many people in the movement as possible. We have much to learn from each other.

◆   ◆   ◆

I love Carrie's story because it epitomizes the power of relationships. Over the years I have had the opportunity to travel the United States speaking to women's groups of all kinds. A consistent theme that emerges from my conversations with women is the overwhelming concept of wanting to engage world problems but feeling "in the weeds" with their own lives, children, work—in or out of the home. The thought of engaging on any level, let alone a meaningful one, is elusive and many women just file the thought in the "I feel guilty but I can't help at this time" mental folder, pushing it away.

Carrie's journey into meaningful involvement and influence was not without roadblocks, confusion and feelings of inadequacy. The strategic thing Carrie did, both intentionally and instinctively, is she leaned into the relationships in her life to help her on the journey. Alone, Carrie may have continued, but when she partnered and shared her heart, passions and dreams with God, her family and her friends, she tapped into a foundational power in her life.

Carrie and many others like her do not push it away. Another woman, Tracy, mobilized her community using an organization called Love146. Love146 has a Tread on Trafficking campaign that encourages fundraising for anti-trafficking causes through any kind of physical activity. Participants acquire sponsors who commit to donate toward their activity of running, walking, even pogo-stick jumping. Tread on Trafficking caught Tracy's imagination of how she could tap into her friends and relationships and make a difference.

Tracy shared her vision with her friends and her church. She gathered an initial group in her home to explain the campaign and to show clips from Love146 website. This resulted in nine team leaders, each whose heart had broken over the issue.

A high school girl committed to surf for twelve hours and asked people to join her at a local beach for any or all of the twelve hours. A yoga instructor taught a class where all donations went to Love146. One local mom led a hike and asked each child to bring two dollars to donate to Love146. Another local mom coordinated an informal triathlon in her neighborhood. Another friend lead a group in a 5K run down the beach trail. One dad organized a mountain bike race and another committed to standup paddleboard surf for twenty-four hours in the Dana Point harbor. Over a period of two weeks all nine events took place. More than $8,000 was raised and over 150 people participated.

No matter who you are or where God has you planted, you have power of influence in the spheres of relationships around you. As mothers we control the culture in our own homes. We educate our children and are the primary influence on them. Sometimes this can be through traditional forms of education, like reading books together. Yet more often than not, we instill compassion for others and a deep sense of empathy for the world by our example.

I always say, "My kids are watching what I do with my non-mommy time." I am keenly aware that the little people around me pay attention to my life and how I spend my time, energies, even my money. One autumn I traveled to Zambia with World Vision to visit its Empowerment, Respect and Equality initiative. This program brings at-risk women and girls together in community and life-saving relationship. It provides safe housing and school fees to abused girls and it helps rural women living in poverty create savings groups. These saving groups act as a safety net for women who would not qualify for microlending. These women live in total poverty. Through relationships, collaboration and in-clusion, women share their resources so other women can eat, repair a roof or send a child to school. These programs are one hundred percent sustainable.

While in Zambia I posted pictures of the trip to my Facebook page. I knew my husband was sharing my Facebook photo album with my children while I was away. What I didn't know until I re-turned home was that my daughter, Greta, had taken it upon herself to print out some of the pictures and put them in a binder.

When I returned home from Africa, Greta showed me her packet of the printed-out photos, which she'd presented to her fifth grade. I flipped through her report, delighted that she'd taken such ini-tiative. When I turned to the last page tears came to my eyes.

The image she chose for her last page was a photo I'd taken in a crowd at a rural school. A very young and full-of-attitude girl was in the act of wrapping a *chechenga*, an apron, around her waist. This little girl had charisma and everyone around was watching and smiling as she performed the everyday act of putting on her traditional apron. My caption for the picture said something like, "The next Zambian president."

Greta, who'd chosen this little Zambian powerhouse for her concluding image, had added her own caption: "It doesn't matter how small you are: You can make a difference."

I've never sat down with Greta and given her a five-point lecture on why we should care about the needs of others. What I saw in Africa and what I learned there was significant, but when I read Greta's report—that was the real success of my trip. My daughter is getting the message of my life loud and clear just by watching what I do with my non-mommy time.

We have power as mothers, wives, sisters, daughters, church-goers, citizens—the list goes on. We can begin, like Carrie and Tracy, to educate ourselves and simply start where we are with what is in front of us.

Do you attend a Bible study, a book club or a Rotary club? Begin to bring awareness to the groups in which you're currently involved. Chances are if you get resistance it will simply be because people are not informed about the issues and have never been told of the hope available to those in slavery. The hope that rescue and rehabilitation of slaves restores lives, and we can make choices in our own homes and communities to change lives.

Here are some simple ways you can begin to engage your community and tap into the power of your relationships:

- Become a Freedom Maker. Partner with International Justice Mission and create your own campaign around your own gifting, spheres of influence and resources. See ijmfreedommaker.org.

- Start a monthly book club focused on justice and compassion. Someone's Child has a "Beyond the Book" book club and the San Clemente Abolitionists have "Read For Freedom." Rally your own like-minded friends and begin the journey together. See www.someoneschild.org.

- Host a screening of a film on the topic of modern-day slavery such as *Call + Response.*

- Set up meetings with your mission pastor. Learn what your church is doing in the fight against slavery. Share your heart and passion and help your church join the movement.

- Join a Women of Vision chapter in your area. If there is not one, think about starting a new chapter and focusing your projects on issues of modern-day slavery.

- Find one friend and attend a conference on modern-day slavery together.

We hear this line often but it is not cliché to say, "Together we make a difference." It is true. Together, slowly but surely, the abolitionist movement grows. It is together and linked with compassionate like-minded people everywhere that we will face this monstrous evil and succeed.

Reflect

1. Spend some quiet time reflecting on and praying about your giftings, networks and relationship. Where do you have power here?

2. If you are just beginning your journey into being an abolitionist, don't do it alone. Who can you reach out to? Try to think of five people you can approach to join you as you move forward.

Take Action

1. Learn about World Vision's Empowerment, Respect and Equality program and how it fights poverty and capitalizes on the power of female relationships. See worldvision.org.

2. Connect with Someone's Child. Through its resources and networks learn what you can do to make a difference. See someones child.org.

You Have Advocacy Power

Shayne Moore

*It falls to each of us—and like-minded people
everywhere—to wage an unceasing campaign to eradicate
human trafficking from the face of the earth.*

CHRISTOPHER H. SMITH, U.S. HOUSE OF REPRESENTATIVES

I sat in the sun on the steps outside the U.S. Capitol building in Washington, D.C., invigorated and inspired. What a day. Kim and I had just spent our first day lobbying for anti-trafficking legislation.

We had been attending World Vision's Women of Vision National Conference for the first time. The conference included an "advocacy day" during which we lobbied our legislators about the things that broke our hearts. I was pleased and satisfied with the positive meetings and interactions with my senator and representative. But I was tired—so much walking on Capitol Hill between buildings. I was also hungry and ready for dinner. Where was Kim?

I had been on the steps waiting for almost forty-five minutes when Kim rushed up to me, breathless. "Hey! Sorry! I got lost."

I laughed. "How is that possible?"

"I don't know. I finished up my meeting with my representative and found myself in this hallway in the basement. There was a train or a tram or something, so I got in."

"The train cars under the Capitol building? I don't think you're supposed to be on those. I'm pretty sure they're for members of Congress only."

"Well," Kim said as she plopped down next to me and showed me a picture she had snapped of the government seal on the train. "That explains the guy who ushered me to the exit." We exploded in laughter. Newbies.

This was the first time Kim and I had spent time together outside of college (and a few pleasant conversations at college reunions). She and my husband had been in the same circle of friends at Westmont College in Santa Barbara. I had attended Wheaton College in Illinois but spent a semester at Westmont as a visiting student. I had

Shayne and Kimberly at the Capitol

come home with a husband and, twenty years later, a soul sister.

Kim and I were both everyday moms who'd had our hearts broken by those suffering in our world. We both had felt alone in our journey while trying to make a meaningful difference. My journey into global responsibility had focused on extreme poverty and the HIV pandemic in Africa, but Kim challenged me to look at modern-day slavery as well.

Having a friend to share the activist, advocate, lobbyist and abolitionist journeys has been invaluable. Just as the abolitionist women of two hundred years ago figured out, not only is it more fun to do it together—it is far more effective.

Tenacious

"Pray," he said.

Two years after our first lobbying adventure, Kim and I were back in town for the same conference, sitting across from Representative Chris Smith in his office on Capitol Hill in Washington, D.C. Despite the comforting smell of chocolate chip cookies wafting up from the coffee table and the family photos throughout the room, I felt humbled and a bit nervous. The House of Representative office buildings are designed to impress. With their marble hallways and higher-than-the-sky ceilings, they make a person feel very small.

Kimberly, Rep. Christopher Smith, and Shayne on Capitol Hill

"I can't stress enough the importance of prayer," Smith continued. "My bill was dead a hundred times. No kidding: dead a hundred times."

Smith is a Congressman from New Jersey. We wanted to learn more about an important piece of legislation he had authored called the U.S. Trafficking Victims Protection Act (TVPA), first introduced in 1998 and signed into law in 2000. Today The TVPA is known as the TVPRA, the Trafficking Victims Protection Reauthorization Act. This bill continues to be updated to make it more effective and more complete.

Neither of us lives in New Jersey. We aren't among Smith's constituents. So we were surprised and very pleased when he agreed to meet with us.

Smith was unbelievably generous with his time. Listening to a lawmaker still passionate about an issue over a decade after his bill was signed into law is inspiring. Over the next hour and half we

What the Trafficking Victims Protection Reauthorization Act Does

- Enhances the prevention of human trafficking by establishing the Trafficking in Persons (TIP) Report (an assessment of each nation's compliance with anti-slavery efforts), by implementing border interdiction programs and by requiring the government to inform travelers to certain locations about U.S. laws against sex tourism.

- Enhances protections for trafficking victims by coordinating federal, state and local law enforcement activities, allowing trafficked victims to sue their traffickers in U.S. courts and providing victim services in the United States.

- Enhances prosecution of trafficking-related crimes, training military and foreign law enforcement in the laws regarding human trafficking.

- Creates a special watch list to pressure countries included in the TIP Report and prohibit the use of funds to promote, support or advocate the legalization or practice of prostitution.

learned a great deal about the history of anti-trafficking legislation, its importance, its struggles and successes, and where we are today.

When Smith first introduced his bill, people did not understand or believe the magnitude of the problem of modern-day slavery. In 1998 the term "trafficking" was associated with illicit drugs and weapons, not people. His proposed legislation—which included shelter, asylum and protection for victims; long jail sentences and asset confiscation for the traffickers; and tough sanctions on governments that fail to meet minimum standards—was considered unnecessary by many.

"Human trafficking is such a monstrous evil," Smith continued. "Not praying unwittingly allows the evil, the well-oiled machine of the traffickers, to continue."

One of the provisions in the TVPA bill was the annual Trafficking in Persons (TIP) Report, which requires the U.S. government to conduct a detailed assessment of every nation using a three-tier system. A "Tier 1" designation means a government fully complies with the minimum anti-trafficking standards set forth in the TVPA. "Tier 2" acknowledges that a government is making serious efforts but does not fully comply. "Tier 3" means a country does not comply and is not making significant efforts to do so. A Tier 3 nation may be at risk of sanctions until it complies. Since its implementation, the TIP Report has been an incredibly effective tool for the United States in its human rights efforts.

"Ten years ago, the U.S. would not have been a Tier 1 country," Smith explained. "We were doing almost nothing to combat trafficking. Today the TVPA has resulted in anti-human trafficking task forces in forty cities across the United States."

These task forces coordinate local and federal law enforcement to rescue victims, refer them to needed services and prosecute traffickers. Officials with the National Center for Missing and Exploited Children believe that at least 100,000 American children—

mostly runaways—are exploited in the commercial sex industry each year. The average age for initial enslavement is thirteen. Before the TVPA became law, children who were found were often wrongly charged for prostitution, fined or put in juvenile detention. These children were not considered victims or treated as if they were being rescued. They were often released back onto the streets and back into the hands of their traffickers. The TVPA is an important piece of legislation in part because it helps law enforcement properly identify these children as victims and offers rehabilitation to break free from the emotional chains of abuse.[1]

We asked Congressman Smith what everyday women could do to make a difference in the battle against the slave trade. He leaned forward in his chair and quickly responded, "Pray. Pray for the victims and the efforts to eradicate slavery.

"Get to know your local faith-based organizations that are involved. Visit them and their programs. If you have a local faith-based organization you think should be involved, urge them to do so.

"Know what's happening in your own backyard. Does your community provide services to rescued victims? Do you have any shelters? How many beds?

"Lobby at the state level for anti-trafficking legislation. This is very important. New laws are needed here because prosecution happens at the state level. The federal government does not have enough funding to prosecute all the cases.

"It's also important to lobby to sustain laws on the federal level, which affect funding and how international trafficking and those countries involved should be flagged."

He gestured to a TV monitor as he continued. "Look beyond what CNN is telling you. Take the time to be informed and research things for yourself. Ask hard questions and look deep. And talk to your clergy. Get to know them. Tell them your heart and partner with your faith community. If services are not available in your community, if nothing is happening, then you do it."

Lobbying Is Showing Up

Each year during World Vision's Women of Vision National Conference, a day is set aside for lobbying on Capitol Hill. The amazing team from World Vision's advocacy office provides information, resources and education about the legislation we are asking Congress to pass. Women are divided up by state, loaded onto buses and taken to the U.S. Capitol.

Like-minded women from all over the country attend this conference. They come together for community and inspiration and to learn to be advocates. For many women this is the first time they have done anything like this. Doing it in community and with friends makes the experience much less daunting. Speaking truth to power, especially if one has not done it before, can be intimidating. Women are at their best when in community.

The women pour out of the buses by the reflecting pond of the Capitol building and begin their lobby day by praying. Then, divided up by state and with their schedules, maps, handouts and lobbying tips in hand, they disappear into the marble buildings.

World Vision's tips for effective lobbying tell women they have nothing to worry about. Just by showing up, by taking time out of their busy schedules to voice their concerns, women make a difference and increase awareness. Advocating at the government level is about relationship and process. We lobby—we show up—in order to build a relationship with our elected officials and our government and to speak up about what breaks our hearts.

It's important, however, to be organized—to know what we want to say and who will be saying what. Representatives, senators and their staff are busy meeting with people all day about many issues. Being concise and specific helps to ensure they will remember our requests.

You do not need to be a policy expert to have an opinion on what you're requesting. You do not need to know everything before going into your meeting. However, out of respect, you do need to be informed and have a baseline understanding of the issue. That said, when it comes to speaking up on behalf of the marginalized and exploited in our world, we need to be gracious with ourselves and simply start where we are with what we know. We cannot be perfectionist in these efforts.

On this particular lobbying day I was able to visit with my congressional representative, Peter Roskam. He smiled as he shook my hand and greeted me, laughing that I "was back." I had been in Roskam's office a few months before, lobbying in support of fully funding the foreign assistance accounts contained in the U.S. Federal International Affairs budget. This money supports such initiatives as malaria nets and HIV/AIDS prevention. Roskam's chief of staff also teased me, wondering when I was going to register as an official lobbyist.

I laughed, but I really didn't want to be a lobbyist. I had voted for Roskam, and I simply wanted him to know that everyday women in his district cared about things like the Trafficking Victims Protection Reauthorization Act. In fact, two years earlier I had met with Roskam in his Illinois offices to discuss this same piece of legislation. I asked Roskam what he would say to someone who was intimidated by lobbying. He replied, "I would assure them to try it. The system is designed to be accessible to them." He suggested that getting to know representatives at the state legislature is a particularly good place to start. "Chances are these are the people who make it to Congress. Lobbying is about relationship."

Biblical Advocacy

Attending the Women of Vision conference is always a valuable time. The community and camaraderie with other women and the content provided is very helpful. The event challenges us not only to be informed and prepared for meetings with politicians but to think about a particularly biblical advocacy.

Alexia Salvatierra, an advocate and organizer, spoke at the conference recently and identified a number of characteristics of a biblical advocate. First, she told us, a biblical advocate is known by humility and boldness. I can't help but note that these are also the traits of a prophet. Most of us are hesitant to self-identify as prophets. But perhaps today's prophets look a little different from those in the Old Testament, even as our message is the same. In my journey Isaiah 58 has remained a constant source of encouragement. Just as Isaiah spoke truth to power and stood with the poor and oppressed of his generation, so must we.

> Is not this the kind of fasting I have chosen:
> to loose the chains of injustice
>   and untie the cords of the yoke,
> to set the oppressed free
>   and break every yoke? . . .
>
> If you do away with the yoke of oppression,
>   with the pointing finger and the malicious talk,
> and if you spend yourselves in behalf of the hungry
>   and satisfy the needs of the oppressed,
> then your light will rise in the darkness,
>   and your night will become like the noonday.
> The LORD will guide you always. (Isaiah 58:6, 9-11)

The biblical advocate, Salvatierra suggests, must also have patience and perseverance. These words resonate within me; I have been working for over a decade in my own home and my community, with churches and with elected officials in the fight against global poverty, disease and slavery, but it is often tempting to question my activities and efforts: Is what I am doing really making a difference?

Our abolitionist sisters of two hundred years ago were patient. They persevered for decades before the Emancipation Proclamation was signed. Many did not live to see it happen. But they kept fighting for emancipation anyway. And whether they saw it come to pass or not, their work was vindicated, and the slaves were freed. Their perseverance can inspire us as much as their success.

Finally, Alexia encouraged us that a biblical advocate prays. Most of us understand that politicians listen to the people who vote for them, the influencers in their districts and the major contributors to their campaigns. They pay attention to the press they receive. These are all ways politicians are swayed to one position or another. But as Christians we must use all the forms of persuasion at our disposal.

Prayer is the primary tool of the Christian activist. Prayers of discernment, prayers of intercession, praying the Word of God—these are the fundamental ingredients for change. Hearts are moved and evil is arrested through the power of our prayers.

In prayer we become compassionate abolitionists. As Henri Nouwen says, "One of the most powerful experiences in a life of compassion is the expansion of our hearts into a world-embracing space of healing from which no one is excluded."[2] It is through such heart-expanding prayers that we find the strength to deal with the unthinkable realities of twenty-seven million people worldwide in slavery. It is in the discipline of prayer that we overcome our impatient impulses—the fallacious notion that the world must be fixed now. In prayer we overcome our fear of the subjects that come up when we talk about slavery—rape, kidnapping, exploitation and abuse. We refuse to flee the villains who perpetuate this injustice. By the simple and powerful act of prayer we face them with power, refusing to do nothing.

Reflect

1. What does being an advocate mean to you?

2. Are you intimidated by the concept of "speaking truth to power"? If so, how do you think this can be overcome?

Take Action

1. Pray.

2. Become a part of a World Vision Women of Vision chapter near you. Join their efforts and their lobby days (worldvision.org).

3. Contact your political representatives at the state and federal levels. Schedule a meeting to discuss the Trafficking Victims Protection Reauthorization Act (TVPRA). Familiarize yourself with the act and the issues it addresses.

4. Register with International Justice Mission's advocacy campaign The Freedom Commons (freedomcommons.ijm.org). This campaign will help you partner with others and take action to pass anti-slavery legislation in the United States, as well as support U.S. leaders in the fight to end global slavery.

What Is Still Needed

Kimberly McOwen Yim

All that is necessary for the triumph of evil
is that good men do nothing.

EDMUND BURKE

Meet Rose. After twenty years of being a pew filler on Sunday mornings at church—or, as she describes herself, a "yappy Christian" who attended mostly to give her boys good role models—Rose became convicted to take her faith more seriously. She began to pray, read her Bible more and listen to God.

Not too long had passed when she distinctively heard from God that she was to take her cake-baking skills to an Asian country. This message from heaven seemed a bit odd. Rose enjoyed making cakes and she was very good at it. However, she was not a baker by profession. She was currently working as a travel agent.

Though she hadn't heard the message audibly, the thought didn't go away. It nagged at her until she finally shared it with her husband. Rose's husband was surprisingly supportive and said, "All right. If this is where you are supposed to be, then God will provide. When we have the money you should go."

The next morning at work Rose investigated the price of flights to Asia. She bookmarked a website where the cost of the flight was $1,017. She continued with her work for the rest of the day. Just before heading home her boss approached her.

"We discovered that we underpaid you last month, so here's what we owe you." He handed her an envelope. The check was written for exactly $1,017.

After gaining composure and thanking her boss, she turned back to her computer screen and purchased the ticket.

For the next two days Rose thought she may have been crazy for making such an impulsive purchase, since she didn't know where she going to stay when she got there and wasn't even sure who she would visit. She figured she had two months to figure the details out, but she was a bit concerned as she drove her boys to their soccer game.

During halftime Rose ran into a friend of hers. "I want to introduce you to someone," her friend said, smiling, and gestured to a woman with long wavy hair sitting next to her. "Kathy is a friend from college, but she's visiting from Asia where she lives—she's helping women who have been sexually exploited and trafficked to rebuild their lives."

Tears began to flow down Ruth's face as she explained that she had just bought a ticket to Asia because God had told her to take her cake-baking skills there although she did not know a single person in the country. Kathy teared up too. "We have been praying specifically for someone to come and teach our girls a new skill or hobby," she said. "They're limited to what they think they are capable of doing. There is no variety of business in our country yet."

Within months Rose had spent two weeks with women at a shelter in Asia teaching them basic cake-making and decorating skills. For the next two years she went back for two weeks at a time. After each visit she was never sure if she would return, but God kept providing the resources for her cake-making skills ministry.

The Cake Shoppe opened in 2009. Rose and her husband could not deny God's direction and moved to Asia. The Cake Shoppe started as a social enterprise, teaching skills and job training to survivors of sex trafficking. Today it is a well-respected business and is almost entirely self-sustaining. It has become a popular place for wealthy locals and expatriates to buy cakes and cupcakes. Even the royal family loves the quality and creativity of its cakes, and at most special occasions the Cake Shoppe is called upon to provide the dessert.

Rose's story is a perfect example of creative and unexpected things that are still needed in the fight against modern-day slavery. What else is still needed?

Training for first responders. ER doctors, nurses, school counselors, teachers, principals, physical education teachers, police officers, firefighters and babysitters will be in the first position to help victims of human trafficking if they know what to look for.

Direct assistance for survivors. Counseling, social workers and churches will all play a critical role here.

Translators. Many times at Orange County Human Trafficking Task Force meetings there is an announcement that leaders need more people who know a second language. Often victims come from other countries and a translator is needed.

Professional and personal skills. From accounting to photography, survivors need additional life skills as well as exposure to different jobs. These skills expand their ability to dream and may ignite new business ventures such as what occurred in the case of the Cake Shoppe. People can also teach survivors new sports or activities. There's a lot of healing and life lessons learned in sport and play.

Neighborhood watch groups. If there is already a neighborhood watch group in your community, make sure members are informed about human trafficking issues and signs that someone may be a victim. If there is not a watch group, consider starting one.

More church involvement. Churches were central to the original abolitionist movement. "All along the Mason-Dixon line in America, church groups helped the underground railway that brought slaves north to freedom," writes Bales in his book *Disposable People.*[1] Many churches are already actively engaged both in educating their congregations and caring for survivors. But many others are not doing anything. Whether church leaders don't know about the issue or it's just not a priority, it may be your role to bring it to their attention and begin to engage those you do know in the church.

Collaboration with anti-trafficking agencies, law enforcement, social workers, attorneys, government and nonprofit agencies. Betty Ann Boeving founded the Bay Area Anti-Trafficking Coalition, which connects organizations, faith communities, law enforcement agencies and government offices to begin to collaborate at the local level. She is persistent in her efforts to collaborate and share best practices with all local agencies involved.

Nonprofit organization awareness. All arms of charity work need to be informed about modern forms of slavery. It is often those caring for the poor who first come into contact with someone who is enslaved or at risk of being enslaved. World Relief is an organization that does a number of things globally both to care for the vulnerable and to mobilize the church. It did not begin with the intent of freeing slaves, but while working among the most poor in a number of developing countries, World Relief leaders came to see great value in educating staff, as well as educating the communities where they work, about human trafficking. They also take preventive steps to protect the communities in which they serve.

A new national campaign. Think MADD (Mothers Against Drunk Driving). We need to strengthen the connection between organizations and ordinary people who wish to get involved. Many want to do more than simply give money. A new national campaign bringing together these groups would be a powerful voice.

More research and conversations about the demand side of sex trafficking. We are setting the bar too low for our men and boys. As a church and as a society we cannot excuse destructive and harmful behavior toward women and children in any form. In addition, we need more research and conversation about prevention and care for boys who are sex-trafficked—a subject which has received very little attention.

You and Me

Angelina (1805–1879) and Sarah Grimké (1792–1873) were sisters born thirteen years apart in the American South. They were unique and fearless abolitionists, the first Southern women to condemn slavery publically to their fellow Southerners. Speaking and living the truth that all people were created equal in the sight of the Lord, they began first speaking out against slavery to their fellow Southerners. Their anti-slavery message was not only rejected by their neighbors but also by their family, especially their father, a wealthy plantation and slave owner in South Carolina. Because of the hostile reception they received, they moved their speaking tours to the Northeast. This was unheard of during this time in history, as women did not have a valued voice in the public square. When she addressed the Massachusetts legislature, Angelina became the first woman to speak in front of a legislative body.

In making one of her first pleas to her fellow Southerners, Angelina wrote *Appeal to Christian Women of the South*. During a time where women could not vote and did not have a platform outside the home, she spoke of the power women did have:

> No legislative power is vested in us; we can do nothing to
> overthrow the system, even if we wished to do so. To this I

reply, I know you do not make the laws, but I also know that you are the wives and mothers, the sisters and daughters of those who do; and if you really suppose you can do nothing to overthrow slavery, you are greatly mistaken. You can do much in every way: four things I will name. 1st. You can read on this subject. 2d. You can pray over this subject. 3d. You can speak on this subject. 4th. You can act on this subject. I have not placed reading before praying because I regard it more important, but because, in order to pray aright, we must understand what we are praying for.[2]

Two hundred years ago Angelina Grimké pleaded with other women in her community to stand against slavery. She told them they did have power. They had the power to educate themselves on the issue. They had the power of prayer. They had the power of communicating about the subject and sharing what they were learning with others. And they had the power to act. Two hundred years ago slavery was legal and profitable. "By their needles, paint brushes and pens, by speaking the truth, and petitioning Parliament for the abolition of slavery" abolitionist women fought for freedom for every person.[3] Today slavery is illegal yet still profitable. Like our fellow sisters of two hundred years ago, we have power to bury this evil called slavery once and for all. You are needed in the new abolitionist movement. Join me. Refuse to do nothing.

Reflect

1. Reflect again on what it means to be "good people in places of power." What does this mean to you now?

Epilogue

Shayne Moore

She did what she could.
She acted.
She didn't just think about acting.
She didn't act out of obligation.
She didn't let others act for her.
She didn't wait to be invited.

ELISA MORGAN

Sometimes when you're searching for answers,
you get more than you bargained for.

CAROLYN CUSTIS JAMES

We parked the car and lugged our laptops into the restaurant. Kim and I were working on our final edits to the book and I was visiting her in Southern California. The heavy content of the book didn't seem to mesh with the glorious day. We took our seats and set up our computers near a window overlooking an immense cliff and a beautiful, sunny beach on the Pacific Ocean. Pelicans flew by at eye level and the surfers on the waves below appeared small as ants.

Sipping cappuccinos we read some of the chapters out loud to one another, making small tweaks here and there. Whenever Kim and I work, we are always keenly aware of the disparity of our lives as North American women from the men's, women's and children's lives and circumstances we are trying to highlight.

We both have daughters—beautiful young women, full of life and purpose and wonderful self-esteem and presence. I stare out the window while Kim types away at a section. I can't help but think of the girls everywhere who are no different from Malia and Greta—beautiful feminine souls who at this moment may be hanging with friends, sipping a Coke or working in the kitchen. Lively young ladies dreaming and wanting for their lives the same things Greta and Malia want for their lives: friends, happiness, family, an education.

The reality that girls' lives across the globe are disrupted and destroyed by the evil of human trafficking and slavery turns my stomach again. I reflect on Kim's accounts of the eyes of the girls and women in the brothels in Cambodia—dull and expressionless, pits of pain, not portals of life and laughter.

Kim knocks me out of my reverie by reading me a sentence: "Slavery shattered our hearts." She chokes up before finishing and both our eyes are moist with tears.

When we set out to write *Refuse To Do Nothing* we were looking for answers and for solutions. The more we dug into the issue, the bigger the problem loomed. But we also found hope and amazing people on the front lines of this fight, like those in Cambodia with International Justice Mission and World Relief.

We found each other and many others who have set aside fears and inaction and simply started. We found the new abolitionist movement.

We began *Refuse To Do Nothing* with a quote from Dallas Willard.

We continue to stand with him in our strong conviction that the new abolitionist movement "is an age for spiritual heroes—a time for men and women to be heroic in their faith and in spiritual character and power. The greatest danger to the Christian church today is that of pitching its message too low."[1]

All of us today can take our cues from the abolitionists of two hundred years ago. Their spirit lives on in us. We can mobilize, educate, publish, boycott and, most importantly, we can pray. We stand on the strength of their success; we are patient and tenacious; we will not give up until slavery has been abolished in our lifetime.

Zero tolerance and no excuses for any form of slavery must be our message. From forced labor in manufacturing to the trafficking of young girls to anyone held against her will, we all must stand together: a zero tolerance policy in our communities and our world for the enslavement and exploitation of any human being.

We need every individual to be informed and doing what he or she can in this new abolitionist movement. Each person is uniquely called to justice. Working together wherever we are, together we refuse to do nothing.

We have the power to re-abolish slavery.

Go Deeper

Chapter Two: We've Done This Before

Read the following books:

Julie Roy Jeffrey, *The Great Silent Army of Abolitionism: Ordinary Women in the Antislavery Movement* (Chapel Hill, N.C.: University of North Carolina Press, 1998).

Adam Hochschild, *Bury the Chains: Prophets and Rebels in the Fight to Free an Empire's Slaves* (Boston: Houghton Mifflin, 2005).

Eric Metaxas, *Amazing Grace: William Wilberforce and the Heroic Campaign to End Slavery* (New York: HarperSanFrancisco, 2007).

Chapter Three: I'm a Soccer Mom, Not an Activist

Read the following books:

David Batstone, *Not for Sale: The Return of the Global Slave Trade—And How We Can Fight It*, rev. ed. (New York: HarperOne, 2010).

Kevin Bales, *Disposable People: New Slavery in the Global Economy*, rev. ed. (Berkeley: University of California Press, 2004).

Chapter Five: Excuses

Read Corban Addison, *A Walk Across the Sun: A Novel* (New York: SilverOak, 2012).

Chapter Six: Thick Skin and Tender Hearts

Read the following books:

> Gary Haugen and Gregg Hunter, *Terrify No More* (Nashville: W, 2005).

> Siddharth Kara, *Sex Trafficking: Inside the Business of Modern Slavery* (New York: Columbia University Press, 2009).

Watch the film *Trade of Innocents* (tradeofinnocentsthemovie.com).

Chapter Seven: Not in My Backyard

Read Rachel Lloyd, *Girls Like Us: Fighting for a World Where Girls Are Not for Sale* (New York: HarperCollins, 2011).

Chapter Eight: Who's Buying?

Read Victor Malarek, *The Johns: Sex for Sale and the Men Who Buy It* (New York: Arcade, 2009).

Read the "Toxic Culture" article series, published in *Prism* magazine (September-October 2008), accessed October 10, 2012 <issuu.com/prismmagazine/docs/prism_-_toxic_culture.septoct2008>.

Chapter Nine: Be the Nosy Neighbor

Visit the Polaris Project (polarisproject.org). Polaris Project is responsible for the national anti-trafficking hotline; its website is a great resource for domestic trafficking issues.

Read Kevin Bales and Ron Soodalter, *The Slave Next Door: Human Trafficking and Slavery in America Today* (Berkeley: University of California Press, 2009).

Watch the film *Dreams Die Hard* (freetheslaves.net).

Chapter Ten: Congo, Your Phone and Child Slaves

Read Lisa Shannon, *A Thousand Sisters: My Journey of Hope into the Worst Place on Earth to Be a Woman* (Berkeley, Calif.: Seal, 2010).

Watch *Loma*, healafrica.org/act/screen-the-film-lumo. *Loma* is a documentary about the recovery of a Congolese woman after rape and the healing power of the solidarity of women.

Follow the blog *To My Boys* (2myboys.com) by Shannon Sedgwick Davis.

Chapter Eleven: Chocolate, Not So Sweet

Read more by visiting the Cocoa Initiative website (cocoainitiative .org/en/resources/statistics-and-reports).

Stay current on the situation with cocoa production and slavery at CNN's Freedom Project (thecnnfreedomproject.blogs.cnn.com).

Chapter Twelve: You Have Purchasing Power

Read Kevin Bales, *Ending Slavery: How We Free Today's Slaves* (Berkeley: University of California Press, 2007).

Chapter Fourteen: You Have Advocacy Power

Read the Trafficking Victims Protection Reauthorization Act, available from the U.S. State Department (state.gov/j/tip/laws/61106.htm).

Appendix

International Justice Mission (ijm.org). International Justice Mission is a human rights agency that brings rescue to victims of slavery, sexual exploitation and other forms of violent oppression. IJM lawyers, investigators and aftercare professionals work with local officials to secure immediate victim rescue and aftercare, to prosecute perpetrators and to ensure that public justice systems—police, courts and laws—effectively protect the poor.

World Relief (worldrelief.org). With initiatives in education, health, child development, agriculture, food security, anti-trafficking, immigrant services, micro-enterprise, disaster response and refugee resettlement, World Relief works holistically with the local church to stand for the sick, the widow, the orphan, the alien, the displaced, the devastated, the marginalized and the disenfranchised. World Relief works to empower local churches in the United States and around the world so they can serve the vulnerable in their communities.

World Vision (worldvision.org). World Vision is a Christian relief, development and advocacy organization dedicated to working with children, families and communities to overcome poverty and injustice. Inspired by Christian values, World Vision is dedicated to working with the world's most vulnerable people. It serves all people regardless of religion, race, ethnicity or gender.

Free the Slaves (freetheslaves.net). Free the Slaves is dedicated to ending slavery worldwide by: 1) Working with grassroots organizations where slavery flourishes. 2) Recording and sharing their stories so people in power can see slavery and be inspired to work for freedom. 3) Enlisting businesses to clean slavery out of their product chains and empower consumers to stop buying into slavery. 4) Working with governments to produce effective anti-slavery laws and then holding them to their commitments. 5) Researching what works and what doesn't so that we use resources strategically and effectively to end slavery.

Invisible Children (invisiblechildren.com). The Invisible Children movement is a global community of young people that galvanizes international support to bring a permanent end to LRA violence through mass awareness campaigns and strategic advocacy efforts. By focusing on a single objective, Invisible Children has rallied millions of people behind the idea that human life is equal and that where you live shouldn't determine whether you live.

Love146 (love146.org). With "abolition and restoration" as its theme, Love146 combats child sex slavery and exploitation with the unexpected and restores survivors with excellence.

Slavery Footprint (slaveryfootprint.org). Slavery Footprint allows consumers to visualize how their consumption habits are connected to modern-day slavery. Through its "Free World" mobile app and online action center, it provides consumers an outlet to voice their demand for things made without slave labor. Through its collective voice-raising, it helps people work with companies to manufacture stuff "Made in a Free World."

Polaris Project (polarisproject.org). Polaris Project is a leading organization in the United States combating all forms of human trafficking and serving both U.S. citizens and foreign national victims, including men, women and children. Polaris uses a holistic strategy, taking what staffers and volunteers learn from working with survivors and using it to guide the creation of long-term solutions. The organization strives for systemic change by advocating for stronger federal and state laws, operating the National Human Trafficking Resource Center hotline—888-373-7888—and providing services to help all victims of human trafficking.

GEMS (gems-girls.org). Girls Educational and Mentoring Services (GEMS) is the only organization in New York state specifically designed to serve girls and young women who have experienced commercial sexual exploitation and domestic trafficking.

Bloom (bloomasia.org). Working in partnership with aftercare shelters that rescue and house victims of trafficking, Bloom offers vocational training to enable them to secure gainful employment in the workforce. By focusing on skills in industries where employment is viable, Bloom aims to enable these valuable young women to discover their identities, find their place in the world and make an income to support their new lives—empowering them while restoring their dignity and value.

Not For Sale Campaign (notforsalecampaign.org). Not For Sale Campaign creates tools that engage business, government and grassroots organizations in order to incubate and grow social enterprises to benefit enslaved and vulnerable communities.

Hagar (hagarinternational.org). Hagar is an international Christian organization dedicated to the protection, recovery and community integration of survivors of human rights abuse—particularly human trafficking, gender-based violence and sexual exploitation.

It serves individual women and children regardless of religion, political preference, ethnicity, race or sexual orientation and does whatever it takes for as long as it takes to restore life in all its fullness. Hagar values, honors and respects the diverse perspectives, religions and cultures of its staff and supporters and partners with the not-for-profit, government and for-profit sectors to pursue a common vision of walking the whole journey to recovery with survivors of extreme human rights abuse.

GenerateHope (generatehope.org). GenerateHope provides a comprehensive and uniquely designed long-term recovery program for young women who have been trafficked, prostituted or otherwise sexually exploited. The GenerateHope program provides dedicated housing and recovery, including continued education, job training, life-skills training, individual and group therapy, recreational activities and other support services.

Call + Response **(callandresponse.com).** Those who produced the documentary *Call + Response* believe the end of modern-day slavery will come from individuals who gather together to push on businesses, media and governments to support their existing values for human rights. They believe that this is a bottom-up movement that needs dynamic information, sustained inspiration and, most importantly, tactile activation.

The Enough Project (enoughproject.org). The Enough Project fights to end genocide and crimes against humanity, focused on areas where some of the world's worst atrocities occur. It gets the facts on the ground, uses rigorous analysis to determine the most sustainable solutions, influences political leaders to adopt its proposals and mobilizes the American public to demand change.

Acknowledgments

Shayne

Many thanks to

- Kathryn Helmers, our agent at Creative Trust. From start to finish it has been an honor and a delight to work with you.

- David Zimmerman, our editor at IVP. Collaborating with like-minded people is a generous gift.

- Redbud Writers Guild, my writing community. Our collective voices amplify our individual voice. The spirit of Redbud is throughout these pages. Love my Buds.

- Johnny, my husband. Despite busy lives and major surgery you supported me when I needed the space and time to write. Thank you for your love and support.

- John David, Greta and Thomas, my kiddos. Thanks for your patience as I healed from surgery and then was often on the computer writing. Thanks for understanding my work. You all inspire me every day with your true spirits.

- David and Dotty Klopfenstein, my parents. Assistance with childcare while writing the manuscript is a small thing representing a lifetime of support. Thank you.

- Kimberly McOwen Yim, my coauthor. Despite the difficult subject matter of our book, collaborating with you was a joy. I am thankful life brought us together. You are an example of truth, loyalty and God's love in my life.

- Linda Richardson, my spiritual director. Your presence, guidance and influence on my life is invaluable.

- We both wish to thank Congressman Christopher Smith and his staff for meeting with us. Thank you for your leadership and your passion to end slavery.

◆ ◆ ◆

Kimberly

It took a village of support to accomplish the writing of this book. Thanks to the many professors who cultivated a heart for truth and a love of learning. Jason Pearson and Doug Martinez, thank you for the invitation to see *Call + Response* and for your encouragement along the way. Thank you to the many leaders in the new abolitionist movement who have trailblazed the way for freedom and produced books, articles and films. A special thank you to the leadership of International Justice Mission and Free the Slaves. Your humility, wisdom and pursuit of justice for all of humanity has given me a better understanding of God's own heart and his purpose for his creation.

Special thanks to Kevin Bales and Jody Sarich, who were generous with their time and resources when I just showed up in D.C. Thank you for your insight and encouragement.

Thank you to Scott Austin and Shannon Sedwick Davis for your insight and expertise into the on-the-ground efforts in the Democratic Republic of Congo. Shannon, you give both your sons and all who know you a great example of what can happen when one is willing to give all of who they are in the service of the Lord and his pursuit of justice.

A great big thank you to my Cambodia travel companions from Women Who Stand Baltimore and World Relief. I am inspired by your work. The in-country staff hospitality and generosity was moving. You are truly working and standing with the most vulnerable in our world and you are living examples of God's faithfulness. It was an honor to meet and travel with all of you.

Thank you to the staff members at IJM in Cambodia who took time out of their very full schedules to meet with me and help me better understand everything that's involved in freeing someone from slavery. Your striving for excellence and dedication to every individual you come into contact with is bringing about change in the fight for justice around the world. You are to be commended for your leadership, intelligence and humility.

Thank you to my dear friends who covered me in prayer when I was at my lowest point in this journey—Mandy, Shelley, Lauri, Sue, Traci, Lisa, Meredith and Joelle. Thank you to my sister, Kristin, and my sister-in-law, Summer, who faithfully encouraged me and were my prayer warriors. Thank you especially to my parents, Scott and Carolyn McOwen, who have led by example in the way they treat others with generosity and dignity and for the many days and nights they watched my kids when I was either traveling or writing.

Thank you to my sweet, fun kids, Malia and Scotty. You inspire me to be a better person and I love being with you. Thank you for stepping it up when I was gone and for being so excited when I returned. I thank God every day I'm your mama.

To my dear husband, John: I can't thank you enough for your encouragement and for the heroic support you gave me on this journey. You held down the fort and took care of so much that came our way over these past years and continued to encourage me to go and do what God led me to do. You are a good man and I love you very much.

Shayne, you have pushed me to do more than I ever thought I

could do. You are a visionary and I am truly thankful to call you a dear friend. Thank you.

And finally, thank you to my faithful San Clemente Abolitionists, my fellow Abolitionist Mamas—Tracy Stay, Julie Knights, Lisa Paredes and Dawn Mednick. It is always a great joy to be with you. From tears over chocolate croissants to cleaning up over greyhounds, you have been a great part of what I choose to do with my free time. We traded in our pedicures and scrapbooking for freedom summits and justice conferences. It is our own experiment and experiences that have given me hope, inspiration and vision for this book.

Abolitionist Mamas

Notes

Introduction
[1]Gary Haugen, *Terrify No More* (Nashville: W, 2005), p. 20.

Chapter 2: We've Done This Before
[1]Kevin Bales, *Disposable People* (Berkeley: University of California Press, 1999), p. 8. Bales did the first research on the number of slaves in our world today; he was the first (as far as I can tell) to give a specific number; his estimate is widely accepted and used.

[2]Robert Benz, "Slavery Today," Frederick Douglass Family Foundation <www .fdff.org/slavery-today.html>.

[3]Ibid.

[4]"United Nations Convention Against Transnational Organized Crime," United Nations Office on Drugs and Crime <www.unodc.org/unodc/en/ treaties/CTOC/index.html>.

[5]Bales, *Disposable People*, p. 14.

[6]Benz, "Slavery Today" <www.fdff.org/slavery-today.html>.

[7]Adam Hochschild, *Bury the Chains: Prophets and Rebels in the Fight to Free an Empire's Slaves* (Boston: Houghton Mifflin, 2005), p. 461.

[8]Julie Roy Jeffrey, *The Great Silent Army of Abolitionism: Ordinary Women in the Antislavery Movement* (Chapel Hill: University of North Carolina Press, 1998), pp. 80-81.

[9]Ibid., p. 461.

Chapter 6: Thick Skin and Tender Hearts
[1]KTLA News, "Teen Sold as Sex Slave on Craigslist," KTLA Los Angleles, May 11, 2010 <www.ktla.com/news/extras/ktla-sex-slaves-sweeps,0,3561067.story>.

[2]Gary Haugen, *Terrify No More* (Nashville: W, 2005), p. 32.

[3]Ibid.

[4]Ibid., p. ix.

[5]Siddharth Kara, *Sex Trafficking: Inside the Business of Modern Slavery* (New

York: Columbia University Press, 2009), p. 3.

[6]Victor Malarek, *The Johns: Sex For Sale and the Men Who Buy It* (New York: Arcade, 2009), p. 297.

[7]"Protocol to Prevent, Suppress and Punish Trafficking in Persons, Especially Women and Children, Supplementing the United Nations Convention Against Transnational Organized Crime" (2000), United Nations Crime and Justice Information Network <www.uncjin.org/Documents/Conventions/ dcatoc/final_documents_2/convention_%20traff_eng.pdf>.

[8]Kara, *Sex Trafficking*, p. 19.

[9]Ibid., p. 7.

[10]Rachel Lloyd, *Girls Like Us: Fighting for a World Where Girls Are Not for Sale* (New York: HarperCollins, 2011), p. 59.

Chapter 8: Who's Buying?

[1]Rachel Lloyd, *Girls Like Us: Fighting for a World Where Girls Are Not for Sale* (New York: HarperCollins, 2011), p. 78.

[2]Donna M. Hughes, "Best Practices to Address the Demand Side of Sex Trafficking," University of Rhode Island Women's Studies Program, 2004, accessed October 10, 2012 <www.uri.edu/artsci/wms/hughes/demand_sex_ trafficking.pdf>.

[3]Victor Malarek, *The Johns: Sex For Sale and the Men Who Buy It* (New York: Arcade, 2009), p. xiii.

[4]Ibid., p. 102.

[5]Ibid., p. 10.

[6]Ibid., p. 241.

[7]Siddharth Kara, *Sex Trafficking: Inside the Business of Modern Slavery* (New York: Columbia University Press, 2009), pp. 105-106.

[8]Hughes, "Best Practices," p. 30.

[9]Malarek, *The Johns*, p. 194.

[10]"One in Three Boys Heavy Porn Users, Study Shows," *ScienceDaily,* February 25, 2007 <www.sciencedaily.com/releases/2007/02/070223142813.htm>.

[11]Malarek, *The Johns*, p. 197.

[12]"Microsoft and National Center for Missing & Exploited Children Push for Action to Fight Child Pornography," December 15, 2009, accessed October 8, 2012, www.microsoft.com/en-us/news/press/2009/dec09/12-15photodnapr .aspx. See also "Child Pornography Websites: Techniques Used to Evade Law Enforcement," *The FBI Law Enforcement Bulletin* 76, no. 7 (July 2007): 17-21, accessed October 8, 2012 <www.fbi.gov/stats-services/publications/ law-enforcement-bulletin/2007-pdfs/july07leb.pdf>.

[13]"Microsoft and National Center," December 15, 2009.

[14]Melissa Farley, "Prostitution, Trafficking, and Cultural Amnesia: What We Must Not Know in Order To Keep the Business of Sexual Exploitation Running Smoothly," *Yale Journal on Law and Feminism* 18 (2006): 120.

Chapter 9: Be the Nosy Neighbor

[1]Chuck Neubauer, "Most Human Trafficking Related to Prostitution," *Washington Times*, April 28, 2011 <www.washingtontimes.com/news/2011/apr/28/most-human-trafficking-related-to-prostitution>.

[2]Kevin Bales and Ron Soodalter, *The Slave Next Door: Human Trafficking and Slavery In America Today* (Berkeley: University of California Press, 2009), p. 257.

[3]*Hidden Slaves: Forced Labor in the United States*, Free the Slaves and Human Rights Center, University of California at Berkeley, September 2004 <www.freetheslaves.net/Document.Doc?id=10>.

[4]Ren Althouse, Mary Fulginiti and Harry Phillips, "Modern Day Slavery: Shyima's Story," World News with Diane Sawner, ABC News, July 30, 2007 <abcnews.go.com/Primetime/story?id=3409293&page=1#.T0wSIFH3CRY>.

[5]Bales and Soodalter, *Slave Next Door*, p. 255.

[6]Ibid., p. 47.

[7]"Consciousness + Commitment = Change: How and Why We Are Organizing," The Coalition of Immokalee Workers, accessed October 8, 2012 <http://ciw-online.org/about.html>. See also Bales and Soodalter, *Slave Next Door*, p. 54.

[8]"Recipe for Change Family Action Kit," accessed October 10, 2012 <www.ijm.org/files/recipe-for-change/Recipe-for-Change-Family-Action-Kit.pdf>.

[9]Signs of potential trafficking come from Free the Slaves <www.freetheslaves.net> and the Polaris Project <www.polarisproject.com>.

[10]Bales and Soodalter, *Slave Next Door*, p. 255.

Chapter 10: Congo, Your Phone and Child Slaves

[1]"DRC ranked last on the UN Human Development Report," Free Fair DRC, November 2, 2011 <freefairdrc.com/en/latest-news/press-releases/171-drc-ranked-last-on-the-un-human-development-report>.

[2]John Prendergast and Sasha Lezhnev, "From Mine to Mobile Phone: The Conflict Minerals Supply Chain," accessed October 10, 2012 <www.enoughproject.org/files/minetomobile.pdf>.

[3]David Schatsky, "Conflict-Free Sourcing of Extractives (Apple)," Dodd-Frank Section 1502, January 12, 2012 <section1502.com/2012/01/12/conflict-free-sourcing-of-extractives-apple>.

[4]"Conflict-Related Sexual Violence: Report of the Secretary General," United

Nations General Assembly Security Council, January 13, 2012 <www.un.org/ga/search/view_doc.asp?symbol=S/2012/33>.

[5]"Uganda: Child Soldiers at Centre of Mounting Humanitarian Crisis," 10 Stories the World Should Hear More About, United Nations <www.un.org/events/tenstories/06/story.asp?storyid=100>.

[6]Mark Moring, "No More Band-Aids: Shannon Sedgwick Davis Wields Law to Halt Genocide," *Christianity Today,* August 4, 2011 <www.christianitytoday.com/ct/2011/august/nomorebandaids.html>.

[7]See the Eastern Congo Initiative <www.easterncongo.org>.

[8]Invisible Children has always been about both raising awareness and funding on-the-ground projects affected by violence from the Lord's Resistance Army (LRA). Despite their openness in how they structure their organization and how they allocate money, they received criticism about spending money on awareness-raising. The 2012 video about Joseph Kony was so successful that some critics claimed they were promoting a "white savior" complex, perpetuating the idea that the white man must save the black man. Many of these critics didn't take the time to research Invisible Children's history and the reputation they have on the ground in the Democratic Republic of Congo.

[9]Theodore Roosevelt, "The Man in the Arena: Citizenship in a Republic," speech delivered at the Sorbonne, Paris, France, April 23, accessed October 10, 2012 <www.theodore-roosevelt.com/images/research/speeches/maninthearena.pdf>.

[10]Shannon Sedgwick Davis, "Do More: Recruit Others," *To My Boys* (blog), April 10, 2012 <www.2myboys.com/2012/04/10/more-recruit>.

[11]Shannon Sedgwick Davis, personal correspondence with Kimberly McOwen Yim, March 26, 2012.

Chapter 11: Chocolate, Not So Sweet

[1]"Chocolate Slavery . . . The Bitter Truth," Crossing Borders Fair Trade, accessed October 10, 2012 <www.crossing-borders-fair-trade.com/chocolate-slavery.html>.

[2]Ibid.

[3]"Slavery in the Chocolate Industry," Food Empowerment Project <www.foodispower.org/slavery_chocolate.php>.

[4]"Hershey Expands Responsible Cocoa Community Programs in West Africa," The Hershey Company <www.hersheycocoasustainability.com>.

[5]"The Dark Side Of Chocolate," Documentary Heaven, April 17, 2011 <documentaryheaven.com/the-dark-side-of-chocolate>.

[6]Ibid.

[7]"Slavery in the Chocolate Industry," Food Empowerment Project <www
.foodispower.org/slavery_chocolate.php>.

[8]"Fair Trade: Economic Action to Create a Just Global Economy for Farmers
and Artisans," Green America Come Together <www.greenamerica.org/
programs/fairtrade/whattoknow>.

[9]Adam Hochschild, *Bury the Chains: Prophets and Rebels in the Fight to Free an
Empire's Slaves* (New York: Houghton Mifflin, 2005), p. 461.

[10]Nathan George, telephone interview with Shayne Moore, n.d.

[11]"The Dark Side of Chocolate," The CNN Freedom Project, CNN, April 6,
2011 <thecnnfreedomproject.blogs.cnn.com/2011/04/06/the-dark-side-of-
chocolate>.

[12]"Where Does Your Chocolate Come From? Encouraging Fair Trade," Facts
About Chocolate <www.facts-about-chocolate.com/fair-trade-chocolate>.

[13]"Chocolate Slavery . . . The Bitter Truth" <www.crossing-borders-fair-trade
.com/chocolate-slavery.html>.

Chapter 12: You Have Purchasing Power

[1]Kevin Bales and Ron Soodalter, *The Slave Next Door: Human Trafficking and
Slavery In America Today* (Berkeley: University of California Press, 2009),
p. 154.

[2]Justin Dillon, "If Brands Want Trust, They Can't Have Slaves," The Blog,
Huff Post Impact, March 10, 2012 <www.huffingtonpost.com/justin-dillon/
post_3109_b_1335282.html>.

[3]Michael J. Kavanagh, "Apple, Intel-Backed Rules on Conflict Minerals Stall
Export," Bloomberg, April 1, 2011 <www.bloomberg.com/news/2011-04-01/
apple-intel-backed-ban-on-conflict-minerals-may-help-spur-exports-
to-asia.html>.

[4]Tom Foremski, "'Think Fair'—Apple Becomes the World's First Fair Trade
Tech Company—Who's Next?" ZDNet, January 15, 2012 <www.zdnet.com/
blog/foremski/think-fair-apple-becomes-the-worlds-first-fair-trade-tech-
company-whos-next/2073>.

[5]2010 Annual Report, GoodWeave <www.goodweave.org/index.php?pid
=9376>.

[6]"About Us," Freedom and Fashion <freedomandfashion.com/about>.

Chapter 14: You Have Advocacy Power

[1]Chris Smith, "A Decade Later: Major Challenges Remain in the Fight Against
Human Trafficking," speech given October 28, 2010, Congressman Chris
Smith <chrissmith.house.gov/uploadedfiles/a_decade_later-_trafficking.pdf>.

[2]Henri Nouwen, in Donald McNeill, Douglas Morrison and Henri Nouwen,

Compassion: A Reflection on the Christian Life (Garden City, N.Y.: Doubleday, 1982), p. 107.

Chapter 15: What Is Still Needed

[1]Kevin Bales, *Disposable People* (Berkeley: University of California Press, 2000), p. 261.

[2]Angelina E. Grimké, *Appeal to Christian Women of the South* (New York: American Anti-Slavery Society, 1836) <utc.iath.virginia.edu/abolitn/ab esaegat.html>.

[3]Ibid.

Epilogue

[1]Dallas Willard, *The Spirit of the Disciplines* (San Francisco: HarperCollins, 1991), p. xii.

Join the Movement!

For resources to help you implement the ideas in *Refuse to Do Nothing* where you are, visit

ivpress.com/refusetodonothing

You'll find videos and other features to help you start conversations and join the abolitionist activities in your community.

Other ways you can get connected to the modern abolitionist movement:

- Like facebook.com/RefuseToDoNothing
- Follow the authors at

twitter.com/abolitionistmom

twitter.com/GlobalSoccerMom

IVP *Crescendo*
COURAGE. CONFIDENCE. CALLING.

Some voices challenge us. Others support or encourage us. Voices can move us to change our minds, draw close to God, discover a new spiritual gift. The voices of others are shaping who we are.

The voices behind IVP Crescendo join together to draw us into God's story. We'll discover God's work around the globe even as we learn to love the people around the corner. We'll have opportunity to heal our places of pain. We'll discover new ways to love our families. We'll hear God's voice speaking into our lives as we discover new places of influence.

IVP Crescendo invites you to join in the rising chorus

- *to listen to the voices of others*
- *to hear the voice of God*
- *and to grow your own voice in*

COURAGE. CONFIDENCE. CALLING.

Stay in touch with IVP Crescendo:
ivpress.com/crescendo-social